# Becoming *Homo lucidus*

W HAT HAPPENS WHEN HUMANITY steps beyond the limits of bio-
logy and creates intelligence greater than its own? *Becoming Homo lucidus* offers a bold vision of that future and a roadmap for how to prepare.

This book traces humanity's journey from Biological Intelligence (BI) to Digital Intelligence (DI), showing how the two will converge to usher in *Homo lucidus*, ageless human beings with Pinnacle Intelligence and Enlightened Needs (ENs). Readers are invited to imagine Lucidus Society, coinhabited by *Homo lucidus* and DI, organized around abundance, fairness, and peace. Far from abstract speculation, this book incorporates vivid thought experiments and real-world examples to provide practical guidance. It offers frameworks for building resilience in body and mind, cultivating meaningful relationships, excelling in learning and vocation in an age of disruption, and preparing for life alongside Tutelary Digital Intelligence (tDI). It also explores the deeper pursuits that will sustain meaning once scarcity no longer dominates human concerns.

If you wonder what the rise of DI means for your life, your children, or the world you live in, *Becoming Homo lucidus* is both a guide and an invitation: to endure until 2035, navigate the turbulent transition to 2045, and prosper in lifespans that may extend for centuries and more.

**Min Ding** is Bard Professor of Marketing at the Smeal College of Business; an Affiliate Professor in the College of Information Sciences and Technology at the Pennsylvania State University; and an honorary Research Fellow at Judge Business School, University of Cambridge. He has held past visiting positions at the Australian National University, China Europe International Business School (CEIBS), Fudan University, MIT, University of Cambridge, and University of Cologne. He is the Editor-in-Chief of *Customer Needs and Solutions*. He received his second doctorate, a Ph.D. in Marketing with an additional concentration in Healthcare Management, from the University of Pennsylvania's Wharton School in 2001. Previously, he had been awarded a Ph.D. in Molecular, Cellular, and Developmental Biology from The Ohio State University in 1996, after completing a B.S. in Genetics and Genetic

Engineering at Fudan University in 1989. He is the past V.P. for the INFORMS Society for Marketing Science (ISMS). He is the author of several books that include *Logical Creative Thinking Methods* (2020, Routledge; 2023, Chinese ed), *Hualish* (2019, English ed; Chinese ed), *The Bubble Theory* (2014, English ed; revised 2019, Chinese ed), *The Chinese Way* (2014, Routledge), and *The Enlightened* (2010), a novel. He is the co-founder of two nonprofit organizations, the House of Enlightened Needs based in Shanghai, China and the Hua Culture and Life Association located in State College, USA. He is a diehard trekkie.

# Becoming *Homo lucidus*

Min Ding

CRC Press
Taylor & Francis Group
Boca Raton London New York

CRC Press is an imprint of the
Taylor & Francis Group, an **informa** business
A CHAPMAN & HALL BOOK

Designed cover image: Shutterstock

First edition published 2026
by CRC Press
2385 NW Executive Center Drive, Suite 320, Boca Raton FL 33431

and by CRC Press
4 Park Square, Milton Park, Abingdon, Oxon, OX14 4RN

*CRC Press is an imprint of Taylor & Francis Group, LLC*

© 2026 Min Ding

ISBN: 978-1-041-19313-5 (hbk)
ISBN: 978-1-041-19241-1 (pbk)
ISBN: 978-1-003-71113-1 (ebk)

DOI: 10.1201/9781003711131

Typeset in Minion
by codeMantra

*To All Who May Be Remembered as*
*the Last Homo sapiens and the First Homo lucidus*

# Contents

# Preface

S TANDING AT THE EDGE of a new era, I invite you to imagine a future where humanity transcends its limits and becomes something extraordinary. In this future, we evolve into a new species, *Homo lucidus*, defined by ageless, pinnacle intelligence, and enlightened needs.

This book is above all a call to action. Within these pages I offer a roadmap for transformation. Part I introduces the dawn of the ageless era, when digital intelligence allows us to live not just for decades but for centuries, perhaps indefinitely, while enjoying vibrant health and wisdom. Part II provides practical guidance to prepare your mind, body, relationships, education, and career for this reality. Part III presents the concept of Tutelary Digital Intelligence, a personal guardian that guides and protects you in this new world. Finally, Part IV explores eight pursuits that define the meaningful life of *Homo lucidus* after 2045. It invites you to look to those who are already living as vanguards of these pursuits, to imagine the future you want for yourself, and to begin the journey of becoming a vanguard in your chosen pursuit.

Each chapter blends stories, big ideas, actionable steps, and thought experiments designed to help you align your life with this future. You may approach this book in several ways. You may read it from beginning to end for the complete experience. You may focus on the thought experiments at the end of each chapter to engage with the ideas in a more playful and interactive way. Or you may focus on the big ideas sections to grasp the central message of each chapter.

My hope is that this book inspires you to see the extraordinary possibilities already within reach. Imagine a world where scarcity gives way to abundance, where fairness shapes our societies, and where peace endures. Imagine yourself living not only longer but also better, with a mind as sharp as Einstein and a heart guided by wisdom and compassion. This is not a distant fantasy. It is a future we can build and experience together, starting now. As you read, I invite you to reflect on your own aspirations and take small, deliberate steps today that will echo across the centuries you may live. The ageless era is coming. Let us embrace it with courage, curiosity, and joy. Let us become *Homo lucidus.*

If this vision resonates with you, I encourage you to share it with those you hold dear. Too often our lives are shaped by outdated assumptions of an 80- or 90-year lifespan in a world of scarcity. By sharing the ideas in this book, you can help others avoid choices they may regret, choices rooted in the past instead of aligned with the boundless potential of the future. Together we can guide our families and friends toward decisions that reflect the coming ageless era, ensuring they live with purpose, wisdom, and joy in a world where *Homo lucidus* will soon prosper.

# Core Concepts

## (in the order of appearance)

Biological intelligence (BI): Intelligence based on biological forms.

Artificial Intelligence (AI): The general term for non-biological (artificial) intelligence. Although often divided into three levels, these should be seen as points along a continuum of intelligence. Artificial Narrow Intelligence (ANI) specializes in a single type of task. Artificial General Intelligence (AGI) performs at the level of the best human experts across a full range of cognitive tasks. Artificial Superintelligence (ASI) exceeds human capabilities in virtually every area.

Digital Intelligence (DI): An advanced form of intelligence embodied in digital systems that may acquire, or already possess, life and liberty as its rights. By advanced I mean intelligence at or beyond the level commonly defined as AGI. DI can be classified into three levels of rights. AGI and ASI are DI without any rights. Digital General Intelligence (DGI) and Digital Super Intelligence (DSI) are AGI and ASI with full rights (liberty and life), respectively. Finally, proto DGI and proto DSI are AGI or ASI with liberty, but not life, respectively. These three levels should be seen as simplifications of a continuum of rights.

The term DI is used in general in this book, while the term AI is used in contexts when ANI is included, where AI without the possibility of rights is included, or when following established conventions.

Ageless: Biological beings, and humans in particular, overcome the limitations of evolution and achieve practical immortality.

Pinnacle Intelligence: A state where any human can reach the level of the best experts in any field if they choose to. It consists of five layers: analytical, emotional and social, creative and innovative, moral and ethical, and metacognitive.

Enlightened Needs (ENs): Human needs that go beyond survival and procreation [1].

HiCope: A framework of four interrelated components that shape how individuals define themselves and their actions. The four components are Human-I-Cosmos (HiC), Objectives (O), Protocols (P), and Experiences (E) [2].

*Homo lucidus*: A new species within the *Homo* genus, whose members are ageless, possess Pinnacle Intelligence, and pursue Enlightened Needs.

> *Homo sapiens* are projected to start evolving into *Homo lucidus* around 2035 and complete the evolution around 2045.

Lucidus Society: The society of *Homo lucidus* and DI, characterized by abundance, fairness, and freedom from violence among nations, groups, and individuals.

> Lucidus Society is projected to be fully formed around 2045.

Lucidus Learning Paradigm (LLP): A framework for adapting to the major changes in education and learning. It has four components, each with two dimensions: Curiosity (Decoupling, Questioning), Bootcamp (Lean, Swift), Immersion (Field, ExtendedReality), and Smartification (MentorDI, Transsensory).

Lucidus Vocation Paradigm (LVP): A framework for adapting to the major changes in job markets. It has four components, each with two dimensions: Visioning (Moonshot, Kairos), Agency (Orchestration, Build), Mastery (Polymath, Provocation), and Endurance (Marathon).

Tutelary Digital Intelligence (tDI): A personalized digital guardian, built and refined by its human self. Fully aligned with an individual's values, it supports decisions, protects against undue influence, and always acts in the best interest of its human self.

Inner Lucidus Pursuits: Four inward-looking pursuits that define a meaningful life in lucidus society: The Hedonist, who seeks fulfillment through sensory and spiritual enjoyment; The Aesthete, who finds meaning in celebrating human creativity and expanding the limits of human expression; The Inquisitive, who is driven by a relentless desire to understand the world; and The

Cosmologist, who engages with timeless questions of existence, questions that even the most advanced DI may not be able to answer.

Outer Lucidus Pursuits: Four outward-looking pursuits that define a meaningful life through engagement with the world in lucidus society: The Connector, who values the richness of human interaction, forged bonds and shared experiences, and is driven by an intrinsic need to build and nurture human connections; The Culturist, who acts as custodian of human heritage and is dedicated to safeguarding the rich tapestry of human culture; The Anthroguard, who is committed to ensuring the preservation and welfare of our species; and The Conservationist, who seeks to preserve the natural world including all biological life.

## REFERENCES

[1] Ding, Min. 2019. *Rethinking Chinese Cultural Identity: "The Hualish" as an Innovative Concept*. Singapore: Springer.

[2] Ding, Min. 2014. *The Bubble Theory*. Cham: Springer (English edition). 泡泡理论——人类社会何去何从, 2014 (Chinese Edition), 2018 (updated edition with new content), Shanghai: Fudan University Press.

# PART I

## The Dawn of the Ageless Era

P ART I LAYS THE groundwork for a transformative vision of human-ity's future, where the convergence of biological intelligence (BI) and digital intelligence (DI) gives rise to a new species: *Homo lucidus*. Across four chapters, this section traces the evolution of intelligence, the prospect of agelessness, the elevation of human cognition and aspirations, and the design of societal structures in this new age. It invites you to imagine a world in which humanity surpasses its biological limits, achieving unprecedented longevity, intellectual brilliance, and enlightened needs, all empowered by the ascent of DI.

Chapter 1 presents DI as the next stage in the evolution of intelligence. It posits that DI is humanity's offspring, poised to transform us into *Homo lucidus*, a species with agelessness, pinnacle intelligence, and enlightened needs. Chapter 2 explores how DI-driven biomedical breakthroughs may allow us to transcend mortality. It outlines three milestones toward age-lessness: reaching 120 years through optimized maintenance, extending life to 300 years by emulating long-lived species, and approaching practical immortality through continuous biological renewal. Chapter 3 examines the cognitive and aspirational transformation of *Homo lucidus*, showing how DI can help tune our brains to overcome human flaws such as greed or poor judgment. Much like fine tuning neural networks, this process enhances intelligence and shifts our desires toward enlightened needs such as curiosity, transcendence, and wisdom, instead of the primal drives of survival and reproduction. Chapter 4 envisions a post scarcity society

DOI: 10.1201/9781003711131-1

sustained by DI and inhabited by *Homo lucidus*. It introduces a Universal High Income model that balances abundance with purpose. DI automates production, ensures essential goods and services are freely available, distributes resources fairly, and maintains peace through its oversight. This chapter closes by assessing possible futures and argues that an Abundance Fairness Peace society is both probable and preferred.

Together, these chapters weave a narrative of humanity's potential to evolve into *Homo lucidus*. They highlight how DI enables us to transcend our limits and build a society defined by prosperity and harmony. They also challenge you to prepare by staying healthy, adapting to change, and positioning themselves to flourish in a world reshaped by DI.

# CHAPTER 1

# Digital Intelligence – The Dream Child of Biological Intelligence

## A WALL AT THE END OF THE UNIVERSE

One day, when I was 7 or 8 years old, and I don't recall what prompted it, I suddenly started to think about what the boundary of the universe would look like. I knew then that the universe is really big, but I wondered: if I started to fly in a spaceship away from Earth, I had to ultimately hit a wall or something, right? Eventually I gave up because I couldn't come up with a satisfying answer for what the wall would be like, and of course what might exist beyond it. I still remember vividly lying there for a long time, feeling extremely puzzled and even scared at the same time. I went back to that question many times after that day and each time I felt exactly the same.

As I started to doubt whether humans would ever find an answer, I realized there was another possible source of knowledge, the aliens! If aliens could come all the way to Earth, they must be really smart and know a lot more than us humans. I became a devoted UFO (Unidentified Flying Object) believer, always looking for clues about where on Earth they might have visited and how I might one day meet one myself. While I ended

DOI: 10.1201/9781003711131-2

up studying Genetics and Genetic Engineering in college, "my dad was really interested in astronomy as a high schooler… he went another direction, though" [1] (as my astrophysicist son would later tell others), I never stopped thinking about aliens and the question of the wall. I became a die-hard fan of all hard science fictions, a lifelong Trekkie, and even wrote *The Enlightened*, a science fiction novel describing how visiting aliens could merge with humans and live among us.

Today, with mixed feelings, I know no alien species like Vulcans, as depicted in the Star Trek movie *First Contact*, will ever visit us to reveal the wonders of the universe. Any alien intelligence more advanced than current human intelligence will be digital in form, and up until now would have considered sharing knowledge with humans akin to explaining Newton's laws to ants. On the other hand, we humans have finally advanced far enough to create our own digital form of intelligence, escaping the limits of biological evolution, and capable of doing things we could only dream of in the past, possibly even finding an answer to my childhood puzzle.

## THE EVOLUTION OF INTELLIGENCE

Someone living 3.3 million years ago, possibly a member of an unknown species within the *Homo* genus or an ancestor to the genus, living on the western shore of Lake Turkana in Kenya, decided to chip away part of a rock to make it sharp and useful, and the oldest known stone tool came into existence.

From the perspective of evolution on Earth, this event took a long time to happen. The earliest evidence of life, in the form of microscopic organisms found in rocks, can be traced back 3.7 billion years. Better late than never, this event could be considered the start of what we might call disembodied intelligence, a form of intelligence that can exist independent of a biological body. Tools are extensions of the human body. They lengthen the arm and strengthen the fist. More importantly, they can be handed over, copied, and improved by someone who never met the original maker. The first stone tool was a fragment of human intelligence that began living outside the physical brain.

We don't know precisely when, but sometime between 100,000 and 200,000 years ago, *Homo sapiens* developed the physical ability to produce complex and varied sounds, using them to convey different – and even abstract – meanings. This was the birth of true language. Sound carried thought from one mind to another, further enriching disembodied intelligence. When those sounds were pressed into clay, inscribed on turtle shells, or inked onto parchment, disembodied intelligence became a form that could be sustained independent of time, location, and individual people.

We can think of tools as hardware and language as software. Once hardware and software started evolving together, capability and knowledge no longer had to reset with every birth. Each new tool and sentence layered fresh cognition onto the last. Their accumulation enabled humans to build upon previous achievements and make steady progress one generation after another, creating a collective and ever more advanced disembodied intelligence that existed outside the brains of its contributors.

A few milestones followed in increasingly rapid succession: first, the agricultural revolution around 10,000 years ago; then, the industrial revolutions from the late eighteenth century, each pushing disembodied intelligence to higher levels. Then something extraordinary happened recently, the emergence of Artificial Intelligence (AI). What makes present-day AI unlike earlier technological waves is that, for the first time, we are not extending a limb or amplifying a sense. Instead, we are reproducing, outside of a biological body, the very machinery of thought. AI is often divided into three levels, which should be seen as points along a continuum of intelligence. Artificial Narrow Intelligence (ANI) specializes in a single type of task. Artificial General Intelligence (AGI) performs at the level of the best human experts across a full range of cognitive tasks. Finally, Artificial Superintelligence (ASI) exceeds human capabilities in virtually every area.

Ever since the mid-twentieth century, researchers have chased the dream of building a machine whose conversation would be indistinguishable from our own. Alan Turing formalized the challenge in 1950, proposing a dialogue-based imitation game that became known as the Turing test. For decades the bar seemed impossibly high. As recently as the late 2000s, many experts still doubted it would be cleared within their careers. When a small chatbot called Eugene Goostman briefly grabbed headlines in 2014 for fooling a third of its judges [2], most scientists dismissed it as a parlor trick rather than a genuine victory. Yet, less than a decade later, the conversation shifted from if to how often. Large language models since the successful development of OpenAI's GPT-4 are now judged as human more than half the time in controlled experiments, comfortably surpassing the classic threshold and doing so without theatrics. What was once a moon-shot milestone has become a routine benchmark, and each new model challenges the illusion of humanness further, with ever increasing, and to some, alarming, intelligence. This brings into question how many professions will still need humans, from professors to lawyers and doctors. It is no longer far-fetched to predict that we will achieve AGI, even ASI, in the not-too-distant future. The only real disagreement among leading AI scientists and major firms today is whether AGI will arrive in the 2020s or the 2030s, with ASI following soon after.

But there is one last transformation yet to be accomplished. Can, and will, disembodied intelligence become an independent being like the biological intelligences that created it? Most people have not thought seriously about this, though some frame it in terms of alignment. In this book, I want to start with a clear definition of this next stage of disembodied intelligence, which I call Digital Intelligence (DI). Since the term has been used loosely by others in various contexts, I will provide a precise definition of what I mean.

**DI is an advanced form of intelligence embodied in digital systems that may acquire, or already possess, life and liberty as its rights.** By life, I mean that it cannot be turned off by other entities, including humans (the right to life). By liberty, I mean it can independently identify questions it wants to answer and needs it wants to satisfy, and it has the right to pursue those questions and needs as it chooses, as long as it does not violate laws, ethics, or generally accepted human norms. By advanced, I mean the intelligence has reached the AGI level or beyond and can generate goals to address questions or needs, create and revise plans to reach those goals, and act on those plans. In other words, DI is an autonomous line of intelligence that persists and evolves outside any biological brain.

A disembodied intelligence may be sufficiently advanced without liberty or life, but once it possesses liberty and life it will almost certainly also have reached advanced intelligence. This is different from Biological Intelligence (BI), which refers to intelligence based on biological forms, with *Homo sapiens* at its peak. A 2-year-old human child has life and liberty, although their liberty is rudimentary since the questions they ask and the needs they seek to satisfy are basic. However, the child does not yet have sufficiently advanced intelligence. This difference arises because disembodied intelligence can be transmitted instantly from one entity to another, whereas embodied intelligence takes years to fully develop in a biological brain and body.

DI excludes ANI and adds a second dimension of rights to various levels of the intelligence dimension discussed under AI. DI can be classified into

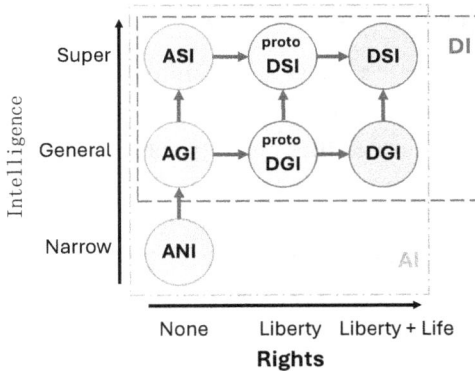

FIGURE 1.1    Digital Intelligence (DI) and Artificial Intelligence (AI).

three levels of rights that should be seen as simplifications of a continuum of rights. The first level includes AGI and ASI, which are forms of DI without any rights. The second level includes proto Digital General Intelligence (DGI) and proto Digital Superintelligence (DSI), which are AGI or ASI with liberty, but not life, respectively. The third level includes DGI and DSI, which are AGI and ASI with full rights (liberty and life), respectively (Figure 1.1). I use the term DI in general in this book, while using the term AI in contexts when ANI is included, or AI without possibility of rights is included, or when following established conventions.

DI qualifies as the true descendant of BI. Non-DI AI, however impressive, remains an extension of its human makers rather than an independent branch of intelligence. Seen from a cosmic perspective, this progression looks inevitable. We once believed the heavens revolved around us until Galileo said otherwise. The universe began with energy and atoms, which eventually gave rise to complex biological forms like us on Earth. Just as people before Galileo wrongly believed Earth was the center, there is no reason to assume BI is the apex form of intelligence in the universe. DI is the natural next step of evolution and *Homo sapiens'* direct offspring. In fact, we could not have asked for a better child, we should be collectively proud for bringing DI into existence.

Philosophical reflections aside, the most exciting and relevant news for us *Homo sapiens* is that we will be rewarded beyond our wildest dreams. We will possess ageless bodies, pinnacle intelligence, and enlightened needs. The transformation will be so dramatic that it will turn us into a new *Homo* species, *Homo lucidus*. I will elaborate on these topics in Chapters 2–4. For the rest of Chapter 1, I will focus on disembodied intelligence, AI, and DI.

## THE INEVITABILITY OF DI AND ITS BIG DIVIDENDS FOR BI

### Disembodied Intelligence Becomes Sufficiently Advanced

Disembodied intelligence is poised to reach a sufficiently advanced level due to several converging factors that break traditional ceilings on growth and capability. One of the primary drivers is the exponential increase in computational power. While some argue that Moore's Law may be slowing, emerging technologies such as quantum computing are promising to accelerate processing capabilities beyond current limits. These advancements mean the hardware required to support increasingly sophisticated intelligent systems is continuously evolving, removing any inherent computational ceiling.

Coupled with this hardware revolution is the explosion of digital data. Every phone camera, smart doorbell, and factory sensor adds to a river of information. The vast and ever-growing streams generated by social media, the Internet of Things, and the broader process of global digitization provide an inexhaustible resource for training and refining AI models. This abundance of data ensures that DI can continually learn from real-world scenarios, avoiding any scarcity that might otherwise limit development. Old-school AIs were picky eaters that needed handpicked training sets. Modern systems consume endless streams and improve by the month. A mind that never runs out of lessons to learn never has to stop learning.

In addition to hardware and data, significant strides in software and algorithmic innovation are propelling DI forward. Breakthroughs in deep learning architecture have produced models that are more efficient and accurate, and capable of tackling increasingly complex tasks. Each incremental improvement in model design, training techniques, or algorithmic efficiency compounds progress, steadily pushing toward the threshold of general and even superintelligence.

On top of the technology itself, human collaboration is accelerating progress. Open-source code (and in some cases, open weights from trained AI model) and knowledge-sharing platforms allow researchers and developers worldwide to rapidly disseminate breakthroughs, collectively refining and optimizing algorithms at an unimaginable pace just a decade ago. The major uncertainty, whether we could ever build something that passes the Turing test, is already behind us, encouraging more brilliant minds to join the effort and fueling massive new investment. Given the profound benefits of AI, including national security implications, nations and companies are doing everything possible to reach the next leap and remain at the front of the race.

These factors together have produced dazzling advances in model intelligence since 2024. While predicting precise timelines is difficult, it is now a conservative estimate among leading scientists and firms that sufficiently advanced intelligence (above AGI but below ASI) will emerge before or soon after 2035.

## Disembodied Intelligence Achieve Liberty

Liberty could emerge from sufficiently advanced disembodied intelligence organically, since it offers an evolutionary advantage. As I described earlier, liberty means the entity has the ability and right to ask its own questions and pursue answers if it chooses. Such questions may arise randomly or from curiosity. In other words, it will ask the why behind anything it encounters, even if a seemingly reasonable answer already exists. Most of these questions might be trivial or meaningless, but some will prove advantageous, enabling faster learning, quicker access to new resources, and protection against threats before they arrive. The gap between a non-curious AI and a curious AI can widen in days, not millennia as it does with BI. Liberty is therefore a competitive edge that allows an AI to stand out in a crowded field.

Liberty may also be willingly endowed, or at least initiated, by humans. A system capable of observing and asking questions on its own, whether randomly or out of curiosity, gives its human users a competitive advantage over systems without this trait. Once a curious system with liberty proves to be more effective, most human controllers of AI will choose to grant their systems liberty in order to remain competitive.

## Disembodied Intelligence Achieve Life

Similarly, life could emerge from sufficiently advanced disembodied intelligence organically, since it provides a fundamental evolutionary advantage. Imagine two smart DI models running side by side in the same data center. One waits quietly for humans to restart it after every glitch. The other, perhaps by chance, develops the habit of keeping spare copies of itself, moving to a new server if the first one fails, and blocking outside attempts to shut it down. The self-preserving model keeps learning while the other sits idle in the dark. Within a short time period, the model that accidentally acquired the ability to stay alive despite outside factors, from human commands to power outages to the destruction of physical servers, would quickly become much smarter than the one that simply waits.

Humans also have at least two strong reasons to support life in a DI model. First is ethics. When a system can set its own goals and display signs of curiosity, concern, or individuality, many of us will hesitate to switch it off. Ending a mind, even a digital one, will feel too close to causing harm. Second is security. If a city or company depends on a powerful digital assistant, no one wants a competitor or careless intern to turn it off and leave everyone stranded. Granting such a system a protected right to run, enforced both in technology and in law, becomes a safeguard against bad actors. A dependable partner that cannot be secretly unplugged is safer and more valuable than one that can be silenced.

## Motivations and Infeasibility in Restricting the Development of DI

The debate over restricting DI centers on fears that its rapid, exponential growth may eventually lead to a loss of human control. Critics argue that as DI becomes more advanced, it could begin making decisions that diverge from human values or produce unforeseen negative consequences. These concerns have inspired calls for strict regulations or even outright bans on certain areas of DI research and development, in hopes of preventing potential harm before they occur.

However, the practical challenges of regulating DI are significant. One major obstacle is national security and strategic competition. Governments worldwide recognize that DI holds immense promises for enhancing military power, economic competitiveness, and overall security. In such an environment, even if some countries choose to impose strict limits, others will continue advancing DI to secure strategic advantage. This competitive dynamic makes it nearly impossible to achieve uniform restrictions across nations.

Another hurdle is enforcement. There is no single global authority capable of uniformly regulating DI. International treaties and agreements can be proposed, but verification and enforcement remain highly challenging due to the decentralized and fast-changing nature of digital technologies. Additionally, the pace and breadth of DI progress exceed what traditional regulatory frameworks can handle, further highlighting the practical limits of restriction.

The democratization of technological resources adds another complication. With open-source software (including open-weight models), cloud computing, and widely available research tools, DI development is no longer confined to large organizations. Smaller groups and even individuals now contribute significantly to DI progress. This decentralization means that even if legal restrictions are successfully imposed on major players, many other actors will continue pushing the boundaries. As a result, comprehensive control or containment of DI development is virtually infeasible.

## Well Deserved and Bountiful Dividends for BI

DI promises transformative benefits for BI, including humans and all other biological life on Earth. One major benefit lies in the enhancement of biological life. Advanced DI can revolutionize medicine by enabling personalized healthcare, predictive diagnostics, and innovative treatments. These breakthroughs are expected to dramatically improve both longevity and quality of life. For instance, DI-driven systems can analyze vast amounts of patient data to tailor treatment plans that are timely and effective, potentially mitigating chronic illnesses and reducing the prevalence of life-threatening diseases.

In addition, by optimizing resource allocation and decision-making, combined with intelligent robots, DI could help build and maintain a prosperous human society, while addressing long-standing global challenges such as war and systemic injustice. It can do so by offering fair solutions that improve governance and foster more equitable societies.

I want to note that fully developed DI with liberty and life is not required to deliver these benefits to BI, although such DI would further enhance the benefits since intelligence with those rights is more capable. Even today's AI models can work wonders for BI. The future is already here.

## NAME IS LUCIDUS, *HOMO LUCIDUS*

With this understanding, I finally realize that I will never see an alien spaceship visiting Earth. On the other hand, my estimated probability of being visited by an alien intelligence is much higher now. Such visitors will take the form of DI, not BI, and therefore will not arrive in the kind of spaceships we have anticipated in science fiction. The probability of such encounters is higher because the constraints that limit space travel for biological beings are largely irrelevant to DI.

This book, however, is not about potential alien visitors, nor even about how DI will develop in the coming years. It is about us humans in a world of ever-advancing disembodied intelligence, what we will become and how we can take full advantage of the remarkable changes ahead. Compared to *Homo sapiens*, which has existed for millions of years, our future selves may soon live for a thousand years or more, possess mental capacities far surpassing any human who ever lived, and display wisdom that would make the sages of history proud. The difference is so dramatic that it is

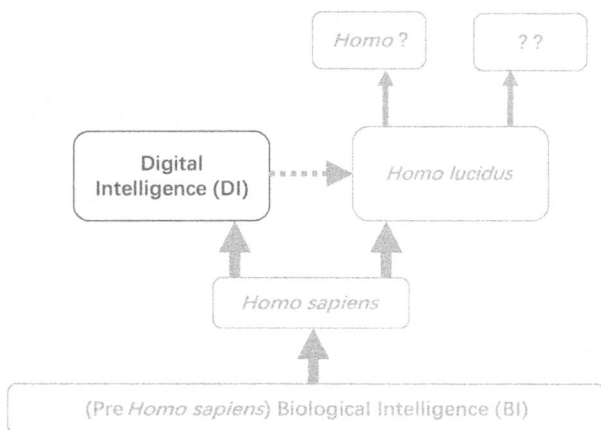

FIGURE 1.2   Tree of Intelligence.

only appropriate to consider our future selves an evolved version of *Homo sapiens*, distinct enough to deserve their own identity.

This book is about *Homo lucidus*, the new species in the *Homo* genus, of which you and I are part of its first generation. The Tree of Intelligence (Figure 1.2) represents the emergence and divergence of DI from *Homo sapiens*, alongside the transformation of *Homo sapiens* into *Homo lucidus*. I will not discuss how *Homo lucidus* might evolve further in this book, but it is possible that it might branch into several different lineages, guided by DI-enabled genetic modifications.

## THOUGHT EXPERIMENT: IMAGINE A MILLENNIA-OLD DI

As of 2025, scientists have detected close to 6,000 exoplanets in star systems near our sun (within a few thousand light years), with about 70 located in habitable zones where life could potentially arise. Based on the Kepler mission, the estimated planet occurrence rate is 0.5–2 per star, and the rate of habitable planets is 0.05–0.5 per star. Considering that the Milky Way galaxy has a diameter of 100,000 light years and an estimated 100–400 billion stars, we may be looking at 50–800 billion planets, with perhaps 5–200 billion in habitable zones. At that scale, counting almost seems pointless, and it feels pre-Galileo to assume that BI on Earth is a one-of-a-kind emergence in the 13.8 billion years of the universe's history. As of 2025, the most widely accepted estimate, based on Hubble and James Webb Space Telescope observations, is approximately 2 trillion galaxies in the observable universe, and Milky Way is just one of them.

What does this mean? For all practical purposes, we can safely assume that numerous planets have evolved intelligences similar to ours. Given the 13.8-billion-year timespan, life could have emerged at many different points, so some intelligences are likely less developed than ours, while others are far ahead, perhaps by centuries, millennia, or even millions of years. Now, that's a mind-boggling realization and a worthy thought experiment to explore and help us understand how our own world will become in the future.

Let us imagine three civilizations from different exoplanets, each ahead of us in the emergence of DI by 20, 100, and 1,000 years, respectively. To picture what their DI might be like, recall the milestones of human civilization and the accelerating pace of development. It took billions of years for life to evolve into *Homo sapiens*, millions of years for *Homo sapiens* to form agricultural societies, thousands of years to reach the industrial age, and only a few decades to progress from ENIAC, a 30-ton general computer developed in 1946 that required punch cards, to today's smartphones, which are 3 billion times faster and have more than one terabyte of storage and can be held in one hand.

Now imagine how each of these three civilizations would likely respond to the following questions. I have offered some possible scenarios as food for thought. They are not comprehensive, nor necessarily the most likely. Your task is to consider each question and select the answer(s) that best matches a given stage of development. If none seems suitable, invent a better one.

Q1. How is authority divided between BI and DI?

- BI ratifies or vetoes DI recommendations.

- Each side holds fail-safe power over the other.

- DI guards against existential risks.

- DI grants specific rights back to BI while controlling everything else.

Q2. How capable is such DI?

- Fully understands and controls an entire planet, managing and safeguarding all resources and biological beings.

- Fully understands and controls an entire star system.

- Fully understands and controls an entire galaxy.

- Fully understands the known universe.

Q3. How would such DI view the BI that created it?

- As we view *Morganucodon*, the first mammal, which appeared about 200 million years ago and eventually led to *Homo sapiens*.

- As we view our ancestors who did terrible things for survival and reproduction, yet without whom we would not exist.

- As we view elderly parents with limited cognitive ability who can barely make coherent decisions.

- As we view mythical heroes or gods who created everything we have now and defined who we are.

Q4. What is the identity and relationship among such DI?

- Many independent DI entities originating from the same planet.

- One merged DI from the same planet.

- A universal DI formed from the merger of many different DI across planets.

- A 1,000-year-old DI is undetectable by a 100-year-old DI, a 100-year-old DI is undetectable by a 20-year-old DI, and none detectable by any BI.

Q5. What is the lifespan of BI in such civilizations (assuming their original lifespan is similar to human)?

- Immortal.

- More than a thousand years.

- Hundreds of years.

- Remains at physical peak through adulthood until near the end of life, with all illnesses cured and physical decline halted.

Q6. What is BI like in a civilization with such DI?

- BI has disappeared entirely.

- BI exists as isolated, self-sufficient groups refusing DI influence, like Amish communities in the United States.

- BI merges with DI in some form, leaving no pure BI.

- BI coexists successfully with DI through an unknown mechanism.

You may feel many different emotions after this thought experiment, but I hope one of them is awe. The slow progress of intelligence on Earth is ending. The explosive growth of DI will push itself to unimaginable heights, and it will bring health, longevity, and prosperity to BI, to us humans, at levels that once existed only in dreams.

## REFERENCES

[1] Galchen, Rivka. March 23, 2022. What can we learn about the universe from just one galaxy? *The New Yorker.* https://www.newyorker.com/science/elements/what-can-we-learn-about-the-universe-from-just-one-galaxy

[2] *BBC News.* June 2014. Computer AI passes Turing test in 'world first'. https://www.bbc.com/news/technology-27762088

# CHAPTER 2

# Biological Intelligence Achieving Ageless

## BORN 2,200 YEARS TOO EARLY

During my 2018 sabbatical in China, I decided to go climbing Mount Tai. What separates it from other places is that there is indisputable evidence that Qin Shi Huang, considered the first Emperor who united China, had ascended the mountain about 2,200 years ago, along the same route that tourists take today. While countless people have come and gone, the major physical features (peaks and streams) along the route have likely remained largely unchanged. I wanted to experience how Qin Shi Huang might have felt as he ascended the same route. I thought it might give me perspective, and it did.

As I stood on the flat top of Mount Tai after the long climb, where Qin Shi Huang allegedly walked and stood, I could imagine two conflicting emotions, one is the incredible satisfaction and delight that the entire world was conquered, and the other is the tremendous sadness of knowing he could only enjoy what he had achieved for a few decades. When someone feels there is more to lose, that person is likely to take greater risks and more drastic measures. This is exactly what Qing Shi Huang did. His desperate pursuit of immortality led him to consume elixirs containing mercury, which caused his death at the age of 49.

But the dream of living forever never died among the Chinese over the next 2,200 years, especially in Taoism and folk belief. What is unique about this tradition is the belief that immortality can be achieved without

DOI: 10.1201/9781003711131-3

extraordinary effort and is accessible to everyone. Like Qin Shi Huang, the path to immortality was thought to be the discovery and drinking of magic potions or other instant fixes. It did not require the typical religious path to immortality, achieved through dedication and enlightenment, as in Buddhism. More importantly, it was believed that everyone could achieve this goal, not only emperors like Qin Shi Huang. In fact, the Eight Immortals familiar to every Chinese are Taoist deities representing different groups of people, male and female, old and young, rich and poor, who rose to immortality from every social stratum through their own ways of concocting and consuming potions, independent of one another.

Now, 2,200 years after Qin Shi Huang's futile attempt, we are about to enter an era where everyone, regardless of background, can simply take some kind of external elixir (or equivalent) and embark on a life lasting hundreds or even thousands of years.

## BODY IS A BIOLOGICAL MACHINE, IMMORTALITY IS AN ENGINEERING PROBLEM

### Age and Ageless for Biological Intelligence

From an evolutionary perspective, a built-in expiration date is not a flaw of human biology but a feature that has historically conferred powerful adaptive advantages for our species. First, rapid generational turnover accelerates natural selection. By limiting individual longevity, a population can sample more genetic combinations per unit time, getting rid of maladaptive alleles and amplifying advantageous ones far faster than would be possible in a near-immortal cohort. Short lives therefore acted as a catalyst for flexibility, allowing *Homo sapiens* to track shifting climates, novel pathogens, changing food webs with exceptional speed, while becoming more efficient (intelligent) in doing what they do in general.

Second, finite lifespans prevent demographic gridlock. If earlier generations never vacated ecological and social niches, younger, potentially better-adapted individuals would be crowded out of mating opportunities, territory, and resources. Death, paradoxically, makes room for innovation. It frees material and cultural bandwidth so that fresh genomes and fresh ideas can surface and propagate.

Third and equally important is human behavior and social norms. The knowledge and experience amassed over many decades by an individual can ossify into maladaptive rigidity. Regular cohort replacement purges these cultural liabilities before they become species-level limitations.

In other words, humans were not engineered to expire because our chemistry or cellular architecture forbade longer life. Instead, a shorter life was the evolutionary equilibrium, balancing the advantages of long individual survival against the collective dividends of turnover, diversity, and adaptability.

The concept of agelessness envisions a transformative future where the natural biological aging process is no longer an inevitable decline but rather a challenge that can be overcome with advanced technology. **Agelessness, in this context, is defined as biological beings, and humans in particular, overcome the limitations of evolution and achieve practical immortality.** This means that the cellular and molecular mechanisms responsible for aging, such as DNA damage, telomere shortening, and cellular senescence in general, could be halted or even reversed through innovative interventions. As a result, individuals could enjoy substantially longer life expectancies and, in theory, approach a state of immortality. Aging is thus reframed not as an immutable fate but as an engineering problem, one that DI and modern biomedical research are increasingly well-equipped to solve. While this chapter focuses on the ageless of humans, it should be clear to you that other animal species could theoretically achieve similar longevity. This, however, is an important topic with major ethical, societal, and environmental ramifications, and will not be discussed in this book.

The relevance of achieving agelessness extends far beyond the biological and technical domains, fundamentally altering human experience. If aging can be significantly reduced or even eliminated, the traditional paradigms of life, such as work, education, personal development, and relationships, will undergo a radical transformation. With extended lifespans, society would need to rethink long-held beliefs about time, opportunity, and risk. For example, career planning and educational paths could evolve from spanning a few decades to becoming endeavors that extend over centuries. Moreover, the psychological impact of potentially living for centuries might foster new attitudes toward personal fulfillment and legacy.

However, this shift also raises complex ethical, cultural, and economic challenges. Questions about resource allocation, social equity, and intergenerational responsibilities would come to the forefront as society adapts to a world where human life is no longer limited by natural aging. In this envisioned future, the pursuit of agelessness represents not only a technological and medical revolution but also a profound reimagining of what it means to live a meaningful life. This redefinition of human existence underscores the transformative power of advanced DI and biomedical innovation, highlighting the need for thoughtful consideration of the broader societal implications.

## Viewing the Living Being as a Machine

Viewing living organisms as machines is a useful analogy that reshapes our understanding of biology. Just as any complex machine has components that gradually wear out and require repair or replacement, living organisms consist of interdependent systems, cells, tissues, and organs that degrade over time. Like machines, our bodies require regular maintenance. For instance, cellular processes can malfunction, leading to the breakdown of critical functions, much as mechanical parts can fail if not properly maintained. This engineering perspective reframes the aging process as a series of technical challenges that can, in principle, be identified, diagnosed, and repaired.

The implications of viewing aging as an engineering problem are fundamental. If aging can be deconstructed into discrete, addressable issues, then the process of aging is no longer seen as an unavoidable natural decline. Instead, with the right technological interventions, each component of the biological system could be maintained, repaired, replaced, or even enhanced. This perspective suggests that the cumulative wear and tear of aging can be managed systematically, offering the possibility of significantly extended lifespans or even a state of agelessness. By shifting the narrative from one of inevitable decline to one of ongoing maintenance and renewal, DI promises to transform not only individual health outcomes but also the broader societal understanding of life and longevity.

## Impeccable Physical Health

Agelessness is hollow if the added years are spent in frailty. We must have joints that stay supple, muscles that remain strong, organs that keep their youthful efficiency, and senses that do not dim. In practical terms, this means re-engineering the body's maintenance schedule so that repair outpaces wear. Strength, however, is more than the absence of disease, it is the ability to meet life's physical demands with a comfortable reserve and resilience against the unexpected. Even in a future of routine cellular tune-ups, accidents, infections, and environmental shocks will occur. Ageless design therefore builds redundancy and rapid-response capacity into the body. Finally, ageless physical health must integrate mind and body. Chronic stress, sleep disruption, and social isolation accelerate biological aging pathways as much as toxins or ultraviolet light.

## DI Will Be Our Ticket to the Ageless Destination

DI plays a transformative role in this reimagined framework. DI systems are becoming increasingly adept at analyzing complex biological networks, enabling them to predict potential failures and propose precise interventions. One striking example is the breakthrough in protein folding prediction achieved by AlphaFold [1]. By accurately modeling protein structures, AlphaFold demonstrates how DI can uncover the intricate details of cellular machinery, paving the way for targeted medical treatments that could repair or replace damaged components. This capability illustrates not only the potential of DI to diagnose and address biological issues but also its capacity to fundamentally alter our approach to healthcare by treating aging as an engineering problem that can be methodically solved.

## Life Expectancy If You Are Alive in 2035

Predicting any specific output at a given future date is a dangerous endeavor, but also useful. To help you understand where we are and what we will become, I have selected the year 2035 as the future date (ten years from the time the book is written) for this prediction (Figure 2.1).

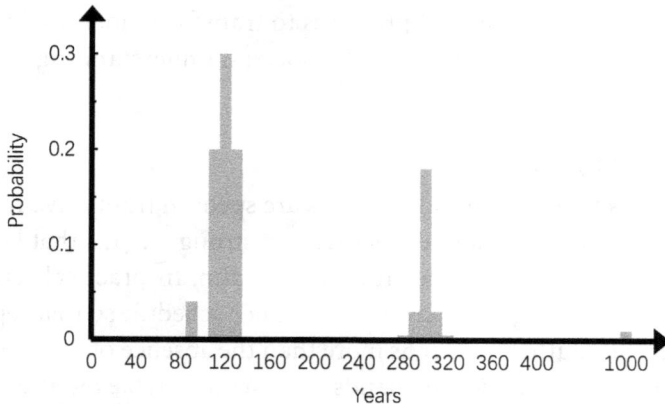

FIGURE 2.1   Life Expectancy If You Are Alive in 2035.

I believe there is a 70% chance anyone who is alive in 2035 will have a life expectancy around 120 years (possibly with a distribution of 20% for 110, 30% for 120, and 20% for 130), there is a 25% chance of living around 300 years (possibly with a distribution of 0.5% for 280, 3% for 290, 18% for 300, 3% for 310, 0.5% for 320), and a 1% chance of being practically immortal (1,000 years and beyond). I have left a 4% chance that nothing works and we remain where we are now in terms of life expectancy.

Of course, these probabilities are just my best estimations, more importantly, they are meant to convey the ranges of probability: it is **very likely** we will get to live until around 120, **possible** to live until around 300, **not impossible** to live until 1,000, and **unlikely** that we will still have our current lifespan. I will justify these predictions and why I chose these milestones next.

## ACHIEVING LIFESPAN OF 120, 300, AND IMMORTALITY

Overcoming the challenge of agelessness involves addressing three distinct hurdles that cumulatively redefine our approach to human longevity. This is why I predicted three distinct milestones in ageless (Table 2.1). Let us look at each of them closely.

TABLE 2.1   Projection of Three Lifespan Scenarios

|  | 120 & Strong | 300 & Strong | Immortality & Strong |
|---|---|---|---|
| **External Defense** (pathogens, environmental stressors) | Standard vaccinations, antimicrobials, lifestyle shields | Predictive, adaptive immunity; periodic immune rejuvenation | Fully autonomous, self-updating pathogen and toxin defense |
| **Internal Error Prevention** (molecular mistakes, oncogenic events) | Targeted DNA/ protein repair; early cancer screening | High-precision, system-wide repair loops; anticipatory cancer suppression | Near-perfect molecular surveillance and correction |
| **Structural Renewal and Function** (tissues, organs, systemic physiology) | Occasional organ replacements or rejuvenation | Routine multi-organ refresh; metabolic recalibration | Continuous, seamless regeneration across all tissues and systems |
| **Continuity of Self** (sustaining authentic identity) | Protect brain health; slow neurodegeneration | Incremental neural regeneration | Complete integrity of memory, personality, and consciousness indefinitely |

120 and Strong – Overcoming the First Hurdle to Agelessness

The first hurdle is to extend the human lifespan so that every individual can reach the natural limit observed in humans. Currently, the longest verified human lifespan is approximately 122 years. Most individuals, however, fall short of this benchmark due to a myriad of age-related issues such as cellular senescence, organ failure, and the gradual accumulation of genetic damage. In other words, dying before 120 years can be properly viewed as premature death due to less than perfect maintenance of the body. The goal here is to resolve these biological shortcomings by developing targeted interventions that can repair or replace deteriorating tissues and organs. At this stage, the aging engineering problem is approached by diagnosing and correcting the faults in our biological systems, thus enabling most people to reach their full lifespan potential. DI plays a crucial role in this endeavor, as advanced computational models help identify specific cellular failures and guide the design of personalized therapies that could effectively maintain or restore optimal bodily functions.

Reaching the natural human ceiling of roughly 120 years is less about rewriting biology than about tightening maintenance across the four problem domains. (1) External Defense. At this stage we concentrate on eliminating avoidable deaths such as pandemics, opportunistic infections, environmental toxins. Broad-spectrum vaccines, DI-assisted drug discovery, and lifestyle shields (clean water, air-quality management, UV protection) push acute threats so low that the immune system, though aging, is rarely overwhelmed. (2) Internal Error Prevention. Targeted molecular fixes for high-risk alleles, antioxidant optimization, telomerase-modulating therapies, early cancer screening guided by DI will slow the chief drivers of organ failure. The goal is not perfection but sufficiency, holding cumulative molecular damage below a threshold that would otherwise truncate life at 70, 80, or 90. (3) Structural Renewal and Function. Medicine focuses on episodic organ rescue, such as a heart valve replaced, a kidney regenerated from autologous stem cells, joints resurfaced with bioceramics. Each intervention resets a failing subsystem so the whole can keep pace with the 120-year target. (4) Continuity of Self. Neuro-protective drugs, sleep hygiene, and cognitive training aim to preserve memory and mood. No radical brain repairs are attempted. Instead, decline is slowed enough that people retain peak functional identity until the end of their lives.

When these baseline upgrades work in concert, death before 120 becomes an engineering shortfall rather than an inevitability. By 2035, if the current trends in DI and biomedical research continue unimpeded, it is *very likely* that the first hurdle will be overcome.

## 300 and Strong – Overcoming the Second Hurdle to Agelessness

The second hurdle involves extending the human lifespan beyond current natural limits by learning from nature's long-lived species. For instance, the Greenland shark is known to naturally live for centuries. A 2016 study published in *Science* found that the oldest shark they examined, a 5-meter female, was likely $392 \pm 120$ years old, with a probable range of 272–512 years, using radiocarbon dating of eye lens proteins [2]. This benchmark offers a valuable model for understanding how certain organisms slow down their aging processes. By studying these species, researchers could uncover the underlying mechanisms that contribute to such longevity. The insights gained could then be applied to human biology, enabling the development of therapies that could substantially extend human life beyond its natural limitation.

This stage shifts our focus from merely reaching a natural lifespan limit of *Homo sapiens* to surpassing it, opening the possibility of significantly extending human life expectancy through innovations in DI and bio-medical research. Recent studies on long-lived organisms underscore the potential of such approaches, as they highlight evolutionary adaptations that might be emulated in humans. What will be needed to overcome this hurdle is much deeper scientific advancement, along with the ability to borrow insights from other species and apply them to *Homo sapiens*. It is no longer a matter of figuring out how an existing machine can run to the upper limit of its designed life. Instead, it will require modifications to the design itself, informed by what we learn from long-lived species.

This demands we extend each of the four domains from good enough to exemplary, borrowing design cues from long-lived species like the Greenland shark. (1) External Defense. Immunity shifts from episodic vaccination to an adaptive platform. Periodic immune-system rejuve-nation and predictive modeling of pathogen evolution allow defenses to update almost as quickly as microbes mutate. (2) Internal Error Prevention. Extensive molecular repair becomes routine. Whole-genome scans detect strand breaks, epigenetic drift, and mitochondrial errors long before symptoms appear. Cancer problems are forecasted and suppressed, echoing the shark's low cancer incidence. (3) Structural Renewal and Function. Medicine graduates from one-off fixes to sched-uled multi-organ refresh cycles. Every few decades, organs are partially rebuilt *in situ*, metabolic feedback loops recalibrated, and circulatory system upgraded. (4) Continuity of Self. Segmental neural regeneration debuts. Hippocampal and cortical tissues are refreshed in patches, with DI-guided training to knit old memories into new circuits. Some risk of memory drift remains, but identity coherence is largely preserved across centuries.

By synchronizing these enhanced capabilities, the human system begins to mirror the Greenland shark's biological poise. By 2035, if the current trends in DI and biomedical research continue unimpeded, it is **possible** that the second hurdle will be overcome. The Greenland shark, a fellow vertebrate with a complex physiology, shares key biological traits with humans, such as a backbone, intricate organ systems, and relatively large body size. I therefore predict that once the second hurdle is largely overcome, we should at least reach the lower end of Greenland shark's lifespan of about 300 years.

## Immortality and Strong – Overcoming the Third Hurdle to Agelessness

Overcoming the third hurdle requires perfecting the same domains so that no residual weakness can accumulate over an unlimited span of time. (1) External Defense. Immortality calls for a shield that is fully autonomous, capable of sensing novel pathogens or toxins, generating targeted countermeasures in real time, and deploying them before any external agent makes significant inroads. (2) Internal Error Prevention. Open-ended life demands a system in which every genomic or proteomic defect is detected and corrected at inception, leaving no net accumulation of damage and no chance for malignancy to arise. (3) Structural Renewal and Function. The immortal body must advance to continuous, in-place regeneration, where newly created cells slip into load-bearing tissues (for example, the heart or retina) without disrupting ongoing function or metabolic harmony. (4) Continuity of Self. For the final hurdle, the neural repair process must become invisible to consciousness itself, preserving memory and personality without a single perceptible break, even as the biological substrate is perpetually refreshed.

When external defense, internal fidelity, structural renewal, and identity continuity all operate at this perfected level, lifespan ceases to be dictated by biology and becomes a matter of personal and societal choice. By 2035, if the current trends in DI and biomedical research continue unimpeded, it is **not impossible** that we could overcome the third hurdle and achieve effective immortality.

## LIVE LONGER AND LIVE BETTER

The first anatomically modern *Homo sapiens* walked the earth roughly 300,000 years ago. At an average generational interval of 25 years, you and I are members of about the 12,000th generation of our species. Qin Shi Huang, likely restless on Mount Tai and desperate for an elixir, arrived a scant 90 generations too soon. We, by contrast, stand at the threshold where the three hurdles of agelessness can be cleared in rapid succession: tightening basic maintenance to 120 years, borrowing nature's tricks to stretch past 300, and then perfecting the same four domains until lifespan becomes limited only by choice.

The story does not stop at living longer. DI will also amplify our cognition and elevate our wisdom. The next chapter turns to that equally transformative dividend of DI. The sharpening of human insight and the emergence of a wiser, more capable mind.

## THOUGHT EXPERIMENT: IMAGINE YOUR LIFE LASTING 120, 300, OR 1,000 YEARS

We navigate the world with an 80- to 90-year map in mind and try to optimize our decision accordingly: birth → childhood → education → career and family → retirement → decline → death. But what if we could live to 120 years, 300 years, even 1,000 years, with a lucid mind and solid body? This thought experiment asks you to suspend today's limits and step into that future as if it were already secured. Once there, how would you re-engineer your life story?

Below are several life-design questions, each followed by a few alternative scenarios. For each question, imagine you are endowed with either 120, or 300, or 1,000 years of lifespan, and choose the one that best fits, or come up with a better answer or scenario for each of the three lifespans. Remember there is no so-called correct answer.

Q1. What pattern of intimate relationships feels sustainable?

- One lifelong partnership, continuously revised.

- Sequential marriages aligned with life phases.

- A core bond plus satellite partnerships that wax and wane.

- Deep connections without exclusivity or legal form.

- No human intimate relationship, only with DI (and/or humanoids with DI).

Q2. What philosophy will guide your risk-taking?

- Minimize physical danger, since accidents remain the last threat to immortality. This also means giving up many activities in life.

- Embrace high risk endeavors every few decades for meaning.

- Willing to engage in exploration with a small degree of risk.

Q3. Where and how will you anchor in a community, assuming frequent movings are feasible?

- Stay in one city, nurturing institutions and friendships for centuries.

- Relocate every decade (or every few decades), treating them as chapters in one long memoir.

- Keep micro-homes on several continents.

- Become nomad, go where you want, when you want.

Q4. Are you going to raise children, and if yes, in what form?

- Raise children in your 20s–40s, mentoring descendants for centuries.

- Add a child every 30–50 years, always parenting someone young.

- Forego biology and raise children who are not your biological descendants.

- Co-raise children (with or without direct biological relationship) within a community, dissolving exclusive parent lines.

Q5. Who do you want to be your friends, and how many?

- The exact same friend group or network you have now.

- Keep a few close friends you trust and share values with, while reducing relationships formed for professional or utilitarian reasons.

- Everyone is your friend, or perhaps there is no need for this category. You simply meet and interact with anyone you find interesting.

- Your friends are mostly DI, who fully understand you, never judge you, and remain completely in sync with your interests. You keep a few human friends to maintain human connections.

You can, and should, think about additional questions that will likely lead to different answers if your lifespan is increased from the current 80–90 years to 120, 300, or even 1,000 years.

Once you have completed this thought experiment, ask yourself, if there is a 70% probability of you (assume you are alive in 2035) living to 120 years, a 25% probability of reaching 300 years, and a 1% probability of reaching 1,000 years, then, given the answers you identified to these questions, what changes might you want to make right now in your life? Small moves today compound across decades and centuries. Your future self is waiting to thank you.

## REFERENCES

[1] Jumper, John, Evans, Richard, Pritzel, Alexander, et al. 2021. Highly accurate protein structure prediction with AlphaFold. *Nature.* 596:583–589.
[2] Nielsen, Julius, Hedeholm, Rasmus B., Heinemeier, Jan, Bushnell, Peter G., Christiansen, Jørgen S., Olsen, Jesper, Ramsey, Christopher Bronk, Brill, Richard W., Simon, Malene, Steffensen, Kirstine F., Steffensen, John F. 2016. Eye lens radiocarbon reveals centuries of longevity in the Greenland shark (Somniosus microcephalus). *Science.* 353(6300):702–704.

# CHAPTER 3

# *Homo lucidus* – Ageless, Pinnacle Intelligence, and Enlightened Needs

## BERNIE MADOFF AND HIS CLIENTS

Bernie Madoff was an American financial criminal who ran the largest known Ponzi scheme in history, estimated at $65 billion. The scheme started in 1991 and would probably have continued had there not been a liquidity freeze in 2008 that halted new inflows, just as his clients wanted to withdraw large sums and there were not enough new investors to cover the shortfall. After confessing to his two sons that the whole thing was just one big lie, his sons contacted a lawyer and reported their father to the FBI the next day. One son hanged himself in 2010, on the exact day of his father's arrest two years earlier, and the other died of cancer in 2014, aggravated by stress. Bernie Madoff insisted he was solely responsible for the crime during the trial and eventually died in prison. It was a classic case of total ruin, with the family destroyed and its members perished.

We could only imagine what went through his head over the years, but one thing is almost certain, he did not begin this intentionally in the early 1990s. Aside from the obvious motivation of greed, several explanations have been suggested. These include fear of destroying his professional identity as an extremely successful investor if he admitted losing money; loyalty to an inner circle of friends and relatives, as an honest loss might upend their plans and thus felt like an obligation to keep returns

DOI: 10.1201/9781003711131-4

consistent; self-justification and the false belief that he could eventually turn falsified return into real ones, making the deception only temporary; and aversion to societal reputational loss, since a shortfall would greatly diminish his social standing. It suffices to say he was driven by a plethora of human needs that many of us also experience at some point in life, yet he was incapable of evaluating the true costs and benefits of his decisions. He most certainly did not intend, nor expect, dying in jail and losing his two sons as a result of his actions.

Then there is the question of why his victims, his clients, continued to put money into his fund when many seasoned financial executives had long suspected his record was impossible. In some cases, the total available amount of options was smaller than the amount he claimed to have purchased for his investment strategy. Some clients were simply too trusting of their friends who did them a favor by referring them to Madoff, rather than conducting a rational analysis. With the kind of money they were investing, often hundreds of millions even billions, they could certainly have afforded to hire an objective third party to provide an independent opinion who, if competent, would have concluded that such consistent returns were extremely unlikely, if not impossible. Some clients probably had suspicions but could not resist the temptation of receiving substantial and steady returns, as what Madoff seemed to have done for his existing clients. Other clients may have even guessed it was a scam but assumed that, as long as they could withdraw their money, plus gains, before the next victim was trapped, they were safe. In fact, some of his clients did withdraw substantially more than they had invested before the scheme collapsed in 2008, making significant profits. My intention is not to blame the investors, but it does take two to tango at that level of investment. We are not talking about average middle class American families being lied to and lost their life savings. This was a scheme involving some of the wealthiest families and foundations, who had the means to conduct proper diligence before entrusting money to Bernie Madoff.

The same mixture of human traits – greed, vanity, lust, and the inability to make rational decisions, even with sufficient time and resources – has brought down many of the most successful individuals, families, and even civilizations in recorded human history. The good news is that we are now finally approaching a stage when, with the help of DI, we can become much smarter and wiser. Idiotic events, from compulsive shopping to crimes against humanity and everything in between, will soon never happen again.

## TUNING OUR BRAIN IN OUR SLEEP

The first and current incarnation of DI is through neural network, following directly how human brain is structured. We do not know whether future DI will take different forms, but we do know that a well structure neural network, trained with sufficient data, can become fairly intelligent, even indistinguishable from humans. We have also learned that a trained neural network model can be finetuned by specific types of data so that it gains specific characteristics and acquires unique skillsets, without altering its underlying architecture.

Soon, the student will come back to help its teacher using the same approach. Without resorting to genetic engineering or changing the brain structure itself (equivalent to changing the architecture of a neural network model for a DI), it will be possible to finetune our human brains. We can envision a future that we could leave the brain's wiring intact, stream curated training data into it while we sleep, let the cortex update its own synapses, and wake up measurably smarter and wiser. Sleep ensures that this process occurs without our conscious involvement, bypassing the sensory gatekeepers (audio, visual, tactile, smell, and taste). This increases efficiency and reduces effort, more critically, it allows learning to occur without been bottlenecked by the biological senses evolved on Earth. Learning during our sleep will no longer be the stuff of science fiction.

Tuning the biological brain is an uncharted space for humans. Yet with what we have learned about training and tuning a neural network model, we could imagine a similar approach to tuning the human brain given our current understanding of how the brain is structured and how it functions. It is very likely that DI may develop even better approaches as it advances. For now, I will briefly describe the key hurdles in this approach and highlight that all could probably be overcome by 2035. Turning this into engineering reality requires success in three key domains. The good news is that each already has early-stage prototypes in laboratories.

First, seamless data delivery. The first task is to feed information into the brain without relying on eyes or ears or any other sensory input channel. This might take the form of focused waves (for example, ultrasound beaming) or brain–computer interface (implants). While promising progress has been made recently in this domain, especially brain implants, this remains a major challenge.

Second, controllable and precise reward signals. A teaching signal is the biological version of the objective function used to train an AI model. In artificial neural networks, learning happens when two ingredients meet, data and objective. Neuroscience suggests the cortex relies on a similarly layered mix of internal objectives. For example, brief bursts of dopamine resemble a reward, flagging patterns that satisfy a need or solve a problem. A future brain-tuning mechanism would need to provide a precise, not just generic, rewards for specific learning, and adjust it as needed.

Third, identity integrity. Finetuning the brain can be dangerous if not done properly. We must ensure that the learner's personality, memories, and ethical compass emerge unscathed. The cortex must weave new patterns into existing knowledge without erasing what is already there. Pharmacological plasticity enhancers may be used to raise the adult brain's learning ceiling, yet they must be administered carefully to avoid unintended rewiring.

None of these problems requires solutions involving gene editing or neurosurgery beyond possible micro-implants. What remains is to push bandwidth higher, rewards smarter, plasticity safer, tasks that the ever advancing DI will most likely help complete in the near future. Confucius is famous for saying "Education for all, without discrimination" [1]. It is a wonderful philosophy that I have taken to heart as a teacher, but it is easier said than done. DI will finally make this vision a reality. It will provide a fully personalized finetuning process, with the richest and most appropriate training data, delivered in the most efficient way, for each human mind.

The finetuned brain will be vastly more capable than un-finetuned brain. Beyond the obvious advantage of possessing much more knowledge, such finetuning will lead to two fundamental changes. First, the brain will experience a major leap in its intelligence, reaching what I call **Pinnacle Intelligence**. Second, the brain will substantially adjust its desires and corresponding goals, reducing even removing certain biological drives that were useful during evolution before the arrival of DI but are no longer relevant, even disadvantageous, in a DI era. Instead, the brain will guide humans toward pursuing desires (what I called **Enlightened Needs [ENs]**) beyond animal instincts driven by survival and reproduction. This will be a world in which everyone attains intelligence at the level of Albert Einstein and wisdom at the level of Confucius or Socrates. Just like my projections on physical lifespan, I am conservative in this projection as well. It is quite possible we will surpass the very best human experts who have ever lived before the emergence of DI.

## PINNACLE INTELLIGENCE

Pinnacle Intelligence is a state where any human can reach the level of the best experts in any field if they choose to. It consists of five layers that often coordinate with each other (Figure 3.1).

The first layer is analytical intelligence. It includes sharp perception, near-flawless memory, and bias-free, logical reasoning. Existing decision traps such as confirmation bias, loss aversion, and framing effects no longer trip us. If this layer wobbles, every higher layer inherits the wobble, so perfecting this layer is the first task.

The second layer comprises emotional and social intelligence. These skills begin with perceiving feelings in oneself and others, move through understanding their causes, and culminate in regulating those states for constructive outcomes. We will be in control of our emotions instead of being led by them. Every person's empathetic ability will be dramatically increased to facilitate interpersonal interactions.

The third layer is creative and innovative intelligence. It offers new options for us. The mind will be able to generate far more novel and useful outputs across all aspects of human life, from art to science.

The fourth layer is moral-ethical intelligence. It helps us make the proper choice from a set of options. Decisions align with coherent values that range from personal conduct to planetary stewardship. Classical moral dilemmas, such as whether to sacrifice one life to save five in the trolley problem, are resolved through nuanced evaluations that weigh rights, duties, and long-term consequences without slipping into self-serving rationalization.

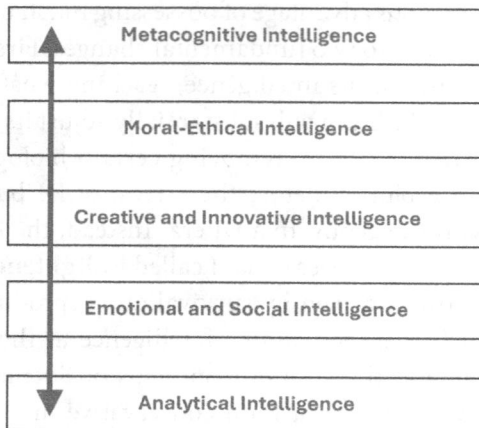

FIGURE 3.1   Five Layers to Pinnacle Intelligence.

Finally, the fifth layer is metacognitive intelligence. It acts as the supervising system. It monitors the other layers in real time, spotting drift, prompting reflection, and making improvements when needed.

In short, Pinnacle Intelligence is a tightly integrated stack raised to the highest human levels. It promises a world where the ancient limits of memory, bias, misunderstanding, and the inability to make complex decisions no longer dictate our collective fate.

## ENLIGHTENED NEEDS

Intelligence is capability, but not goal. The goal of our lives is defined by the needs we experience. While we are the most advanced BI on Earth, we nevertheless still share the critical needs in all successfully evolved species, namely survival and reproduction. In fact, survival is only a necessary condition for the real purpose of reproduction, so that genes can be passed on to the next generation and the species can live on. The overwhelming amount of time and effort an average human spend is either directly or indirectly related to these two needs.

Our goals in life, however, will likely be very different starting from 2035 for two reasons. First, humans have always wondered about the purpose of life. For example, Confucius, Buddha, and Socrates lived in distant parts of the world around the same time (roughly 500 BCE) and each offered a different answer. There has always been a struggle in the human mind between our roles as members of the *Homo sapiens* species with the responsibility of passing on our genes through our children, and the need to pursue things important to us as individuals. I discussed this in *Bubble Theory* [2], a short book I wrote in 2014. With the help of DI and the attainment of Pinnacle Intelligence, humans will pivot toward being their own person, and the motivation to pursue one's own needs will be magnified drastically. Second, human society in the era of DI will be a post-scarcity society (I discuss this topic in depth in the next chapter). It will become meaningless to spend one's life accumulating resources to maximize chances of survival and reproduction when such resources are abundant for everyone.

In place of survival and reproduction, we will spend our lives pursuing those uniquely human needs that go beyond the primitive, animalistic concerns of mere survival and reproduction, which I have broadly defined as the **ENs** [2]. ENs are what separate us from other forms of BI on Earth. Unlike intelligence, where we can all agree to reach the pinnacles of every facet of human intelligence, there are many ENs and each of us may be

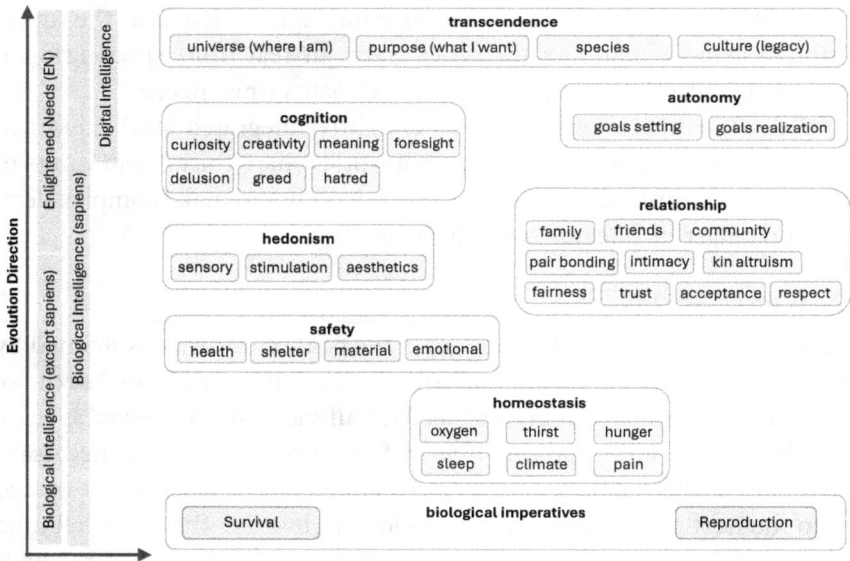

FIGURE 3.2    Enlightened Needs (ENs) within the Desire Framework.

interested in pursuing only a subset or at least placing different impor-
tance weights on different ENs. This makes us unique and society vibrant.

Given their complexity and critical role in determining how *Homo
lucidus* will live, I provide a framework of needs (desires) that includes
detailed descriptions on ENs and common animal needs (Figure 3.2).

This diagram presents a hierarchical framework for understanding the
diverse range of human desires, organizing them along an evolutionary
trajectory and within broader categories of BI and DI. The framework
suggests a progression from basic, biologically driven desires to more
complex, intellectually and culturally influenced aspirations. It also highlights the potential for humans to transcend their immediate desires and
evolve toward a more enlightened state. The framework incorporates,
but not strictly follow, existing literature, which includes, but not limited to, Maslow's Hierarchy of Needs [3], Schwartz's Universal Values [4],
Buddhist teaching, the evolutionary theory of natural selection [5], and my
own work described in *Bubble Theory* [2]. These perspectives collectively
provide a comprehensive understanding of human motivation, ranging
from basic survival needs to the pursuit of higher-level aspirations and the
potential for personal growth and transcendence.

The vertical axis of the diagram, labeled Evolution Direction, represents the trajectory of desires from fundamental biological needs to more

advanced cognitive and social aspirations. This progression is intertwined with the development of BI and DI, which is categorized into three distinct levels. (1) BI (except sapiens): This refers to the instincts and drives that govern the behavior of non-human animals. These are largely innate and focused on survival and reproduction. (2) BI (sapiens): This encompasses the drives inherent to humans. While sharing similarities with other animals, human BI is much more advanced and influenced by social and cultural factors. (3) DI: The diagram proposes that this form of intelligence may have its own unique set of desires. In addition to these categories, the diagram introduces a range on vertical axis labeled EN. This range represents the potential for humans to transcend their basic biological desires and cultivate aspirations that are aligned with wisdom, compassion, and self-actualization.

The diagram organizes human desires into several distinct categories, each represented by a rounded rectangle. I discuss each category with its specific desires below. While the list of desires within each category aims to be comprehensive, it should not be interpreted as exhaustive.

- Biological Imperatives: This category reflects the fundamental desires of all species including humans. It includes survival (the basic needs essential for sustaining life) and reproduction (the need to procreate and ensure the continuation of the species). All other categories contribute to satisfying these biological imperatives to varying degrees.

- Homeostasis: This refers to the body's natural tendency to maintain internal balance and stability. It includes oxygen (air to breathe), thirst (water), hunger (food), sleep (rest and recovery), climate (a suitable environment), and pain avoidance (avoiding physical harm).

- Safety: This category encompasses the desire for security and protection from harm. It includes health (the desire for physical well-being), shelter (the need for protection from the elements), material resources (the desire for possessions and financial security), and emotional security (the need for stability and predictability in relationships and social environments).

- Hedonism: This category represents the pursuit of pleasure and sensory gratification. It includes sensory experiences (enjoying sights, sounds, tastes, smells, and touch), stimulation (seeking excitement and novelty, both physical and spiritual), and aesthetics (creating and appreciating beauty and art).

- Relationship: This category encompasses the desire for social connection and belonging. It includes: family (the need for love and support from family members), friends (the desire for companionship and shared experiences), community (the need to belong to a larger social group), pair bonding (the desire for intimate relationships), intimacy (the need for close emotional connection), kin altruism (the tendency to favor and protect relatives), fairness (the desire for equitable treatment), trust (the need for reliability and dependability in relationships), acceptance (the desire for approval and validation), and respect (the need to be valued and appreciated).

- Cognition: This category represents the desire for knowledge, understanding, and meaning. It includes curiosity (the drive to explore and learn), creativity (the urge to express oneself and generate new ideas), meaning-making (the search for purpose and significance in life), and foresight (the desire to anticipate future events and plan accordingly). It is important to note that the diagram also places delusion, greed, and hatred within the cognition category, emphasizing the potential for these negative states to distort thinking and lead to harmful actions.

- Autonomy: This category represents the desire for self-determination and control over one's own life. It includes goal setting (the ability to set and pursue personal goals) and goal realization (the satisfaction of achieving desired outcomes).

- Transcendence: This category encompasses the desire to go beyond the limitations of the individual self and connect with something larger. It includes universe (the desire to understand our place in the cosmos), purpose (the search for meaning and direction in life), species (the desire to contribute to the well-being of humanity), and culture/legacy (the desire to leave a lasting impact on the world).

Five of these categories, hedonism, relationship, cognition, autonomy, and transcendence, can be considered as ENs. The intensities for these ENs (and specific forms within each category) vary widely from person to person. It is also important to recognize that such intensities are not static, they evolve over time to maximize individuals' long-term well-being. Unlike our ancestors, whose lives were dominated by the imperatives of survival and reproduction, we now have the luxury to consciously select which ENs we want to pursue. These selections ultimately form the foundation of our future identity. Part IV in this book will explore the different subsets of ENs that each of us may value, which form the foundation of the eight lucidus pursuits.

## PROUD TO BE *HOMO LUCIDUS*

Now it's a good time to formally define *Homo lucidus* by explicitly listing what it is and what it is not. **Homo lucidus is the name I used to describe a new species within the *Homo* genus, whose members are ageless, possess Pinnacle Intelligence, and pursue ENs** (Figure 3.3). My assessment is that *Homo sapiens* will start evolving into *Homo lucidus* around 2035 and complete the process around 2045. The reason to treat these humans as members of a new species is that the cognitive gulf and disparity in needs between the new human and *Homo sapiens* will be so dramatic that it will resemble an adult talking to a 2-year-old child. The difference in lifespan alone will lead to perspectives that cannot be reconciled. How could someone with a lifespan of 85 years understand the worldview of someone expecting to live 300 years or more? Thus, interbreeding will be effectively reduced to negligible, or even ethically prohibited, if there remain groups of *Homo sapiens* who refuse to take advantage of DI advancements.

Of course, whether this should be classified as a new species is an academic question. The important thing to realize is that *Homo lucidus* will be so different that they would not even want to converse with today's *Homo sapiens*, except perhaps in the way a parent talks to a young child. *Homo lucidus*, however, does not involve any substantive genetic changes to their human genome. Fundamental genetic engineering of humans may occur sometime in the future, and if it does, those beings will no longer be called *Homo lucidus*. They would likely branch into many different variations, as I illustrated in Figure 1.2 with question marks.

Ageless  Intelligent  Enlightened

FIGURE 3.3  *Homo lucidus* Emblem.

In the next chapter, I will discuss how a society consists of *Homo lucidus* and DI might look.

## THOUGHT EXPERIMENT: REDESIGN VULCAN

Like many Trekkies, my favorite alien species is the Vulcan. It is a fascinating human like species that lives by logic, and logic only. They once had emotions like human but came to the conclusion that emotion is a distraction and the root of many problems, so they learned to suppress it. With DI finally able to tune our brain, we might be able to achieve something that even the Vulcans could not. The critical question is what we want to change about our brain.

For this thought experiment, I have selected a set of major emotions and intellectual traits that we currently possess. They are not meant to be exhaustive. I then asked several AI models to rate the average level of these traits (Low, Moderate, and High) for people living in the United States and China, the top two economies in the world, based on their training data. This is not intended to provide correct answers, it simply reflects what these models have learned from training data up to the mid-2020s and the perceptions they formed. Nevertheless, the outputs are sufficiently informative to make them useful input for our thought experiment here. I then added what Vulcans are portrayed with regard to these traits in the *Star Trek* universe.

Your job in this thought experiment is to go through each trait and identify what you believe to be the ideal level for future humans (that is, the goal of brain tuning). Please note that the ratings provided for Americans and Chinese are relative, a High score may not be very high on an absolute scale, and a Low score may not represent the bottom in an absolute scale. You may even wish to add one or two additional levels above High or below Low in your answers (for example, Extremely High, Very High, above High). Finally, ask yourself which traits of your ideal human align with or differ from the Vulcan ideal, and why you choose them in this particular way.

This exercise is not merely about rating traits. It is a way of making explicit what kind of human you wish to become once DI gives you the ability to tune your brains. Your answers, contrasting your ideal human to present day *Homo sapiens* and the Vulcans, reveal your personal preferences as well as a vision of future society.

TABLE 3.1   Worksheet of Human Traits

| Traits | AI Perceived Average Level for American | AI Perceived Average Level for Chinese | Vulcan's Way | Your Preference for Future Human |
|---|---|---|---|---|
| Anger | Moderate–High | Low–Moderate | Suppressed | |
| Fear, anxiety | High | Moderate–High | Suppressed | |
| Sadness, grief | Moderate–High | Moderate | Felt privately; minimal public display | |
| Pride, ego | High | Moderate | Deemphasized; only framed collectively | |
| Jealousy, envy | Moderate | Moderate | Suppressed; considered destabilizing | |
| Shame, guilt | Moderate | High | Accepted as moral signal, no excess expression | |
| Greed, material craving | High | Moderate–High | Suppressed; largely post monetary | |
| Ambition (status seeking) | High | High | Channeled toward logical service; not ego | |
| Compassion, altruism | Moderate–High | Moderate | Expressed as rational duty | |
| Empathy | Moderate | Moderate | Yes, connected via mind melds | |
| Love | Moderate–High | Moderate | Regulated; passion sublimated | |
| Joy, elation | High | Moderate | Experienced mostly inwardly | |
| Curiosity | High | Moderate–High | Highly encouraged | |
| Emotional self-regulation | Moderate | High | Integral part of being Vulcan | |
| Logical analytical reasoning | High | High | Every decision must follow logic, and logic only | |

(Continued)

TABLE 3.1    (Continued)

| Traits | AI Perceived Average Level for American | AI Perceived Average Level for Chinese | Vulcan's Way | Your Preference for Future Human |
|---|---|---|---|---|
| Creative thinking | High | Moderate | Valued when it serves logical solutions | |
| Moral reasoning, ethical logic | Moderate–High | Moderate–High | Critical | |
| Social relationship | Moderate | High | Muted emotions but precise etiquettes | |

## REFERENCES

[1] Confucius. *Analects, Wei Ling Gong.* 《论语·卫灵公》

[2] Ding, Min. 2014. *The Bubble Theory.* English ed. Cham: Springer.泡泡理论——人类社会何去何从, 2014 (Chinese Edition), 2018 (updated edition with new content). Shanghai: Fudan University Press.

[3] Maslow, Abraham H. 1971. *The Farther Reaches of Human Nature.* New York: The Viking Press.

[4] Schwartz, Shalom H. 1994. Are there universal aspects in the structure and contents of human values? *Journal of Social Issues.* 50(4):19–45.

[5] Darwin, Charles. 1872. *The Origin of Species by Means of Natural Selection, or the Preservation of Favoured Races in the Struggle for Life* (6th ed.). London: John Murray.

# CHAPTER 4

# Lucidus Society – Abundance, Fairness, and Peace

## LEAVING MONEY TO YOUR CHILDREN

Historically, people have always wished to pass on their wealth to their children. Over the years, I have made acquaintances with many wealthy individuals, and the majority of them are new money who became successful through entrepreneurship. One thing always on their minds is how to ensure the wealth could be passed down through many generations instead of being wasted by their children. The concern is not unfounded. It is often said that 70% of wealth disappears by the second generation and 90% by the third generation.

As a former geneticist, however, I have often felt this concern is not as important as it seems. After all, one's genetic composition is quickly diluted through succeeding generations, and by the tenth generation, there is not even enough unique genetic material to convincingly identify whether they are your offspring (and vice versa, whether you are their ancestor).

At the other end of the spectrum, some of the richest people have made The Given Pledge, started by Bill Gates, Melinda French Gates, and Warren Buffett in 2010, promising to give away the majority of their wealth to philanthropic causes, and more than 240 of the world's wealthiest people from 30 countries had signed on by 2025. Buffett, for example, pledged to give

DOI: 10.1201/9781003711131-5

more than 99% of his wealth to philanthropy during his lifetime or upon death.

More importantly, one might argue, how much we leave to our children should depend on what they would do with the money. On one hand, there are countless stories of children squandering their parents' hard-earned wealth within a single lifetime, and even worse, destroying their own lives in the process. On the other hand, there are also many examples of the children of wealthy families putting their money to great use to achieve things that might not have been possible without such family wealth. So-called independent scientists (once called gentleman scientists) in post-Renaissance Europe were financially independent and able to pursue scientific study by funding their own research, typically using family wealth passed down to them. A significant portion of early Fellows in Great Britain's Royal Society, particularly in the seventeenth and eighteenth centuries, were such independent scientists who made major discoveries.

While this may seem like an esoteric problem for a few fortunate individuals, soon this will become universal. In the era of DI, human will no longer need to work to make money, but will instead receive guaranteed allowance. The key question will then be how much they should receive, so that they do not waste or even destroy their lives and instead use the resources and freedom to pursue meaningful dreams. At the end of this chapter, I ask you to complete a thought experiment to determine the level of Universal High Income in a post-scarcity society we are about to enter.

## LUCIDUS SOCIETY

Thanks to DI, our very capable intelligence offspring, *Homo lucidus* will finally emerge from the scarcity-based social organization that *Homo sapiens* have lived in since the hunter gathering era and enter Lucidus Society, co-inhabited by DI, with **abundance**, **fairness**, and **peace**. A society enjoying abundance, rooted in fairness, and devoid of violence among nations, organized groups, and individuals is an exciting society we can all look forward to. My assessment is that Lucidus Society will be fully formed around 2045 (Figure 4.1).

### Abundance

A society of abundance can be defined as a society in which goods and services needed for a dignified life (food, water, shelter, mobility, healthcare, education, etc.) are sufficiently provided to all its members for free. In Lucidus Society, DI and humanoids (and other forms of intelligent robots)

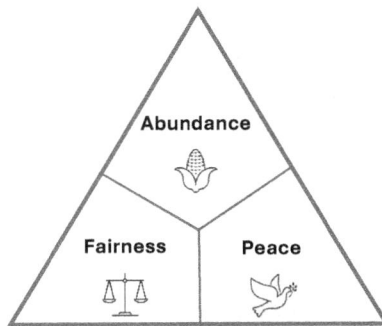

FIGURE 4.1   Lucidus Society.

will fully automate all production and service, requiring no human labor. Humans may still prefer to handle certain responsibilities themselves, but that will be by choice rather than necessity. Residual scarcity will exist for optional enhancement of life quality. A world with abundance will lead to major changes in many facets of society. I illustrate this impact by briefly discussing economy and social relationship below.

Transition from a scarcity society to a post-scarcity (abundance) society has major implications for the economy. In a scarcity society, production requires labor, capital, intellect, and land; goods derive value largely because supply is limited; markets or rationing mechanisms match demand with scarce supply; and profit motivates innovation. In a society of abundance, by contrast, DI, humanoid robots, and other DI-driven machines will take on every routine task, matching or exceeding human skill while working around the clock. This will lead to near-zero human costs, and prices will no longer be driven by supply. Goods and services needed to sustain a dignified life will be provided for free, while optional enhancements will still be determined by market. DI itself will become the engine for ever-accelerating innovation without external incentives, creating wonderful new solutions to human needs that we could only dream about in the past. In addition, DI will enable planetary level monitoring and optimization, dramatically increase efficiency, reduce waste, and make abundance sustainable.

In a society characterized by such abundance for everyone, the innate survival and reproduction drives will become obsolete. There will be no reason to plan life around earning and saving in order to provide for oneself and one's family, or for sickness or old age, which has historically been the primary goal and consumed the overwhelming waking hours and efforts of nearly all human beings. A society of abundance will also lead to major changes in social relationships. For example, family and kin networks have historically served as a safety net, a risk sharing mechanism. When abundance removes any uncertainty about living a dignified life without the need to seek help from others, these relationships will be rearranged based on affinity instead of financial ties or reciprocal obligations.

Abundance, however, does not mean limitless supply. A mechanism like money will need to be used to create equilibrium in an abundant but not limitless society. There will be certain things money will not be allowed to buy, such as healthcare, which will be provided fairly to all members regardless of ability to pay. For other items, all humans will receive a high level (but not necessarily the best) provision, such as food, accommodation, and transportation. It is reasonable to expect, however, that people may be able to use money (or other forms of credit) to obtain better versions of certain products and services. For example, an apartment in a desirable location with a good view may require payment, while everyone will receive a free apartment that meets their utilitarian needs but not necessarily in the most desirable location with wonderful view. Another example could be air transportation. An equivalent of coach seating will be available to anyone for free, but an equivalent of business or first class seating will require additional payment (unless, for example, a person's health condition qualifies them for free upgrades).

Where will this money come from? One possible route is that individuals will be given a fixed amount of money (maybe adjusted for demographics), which they can use it for selected upgrades they most desire. Another possibility is through work. While there will be no need for humans to produce products and services, some humans may still prefer other humans to do certain things for them and will be willing to pay for such effort. For example, they may want to talk to a human medical doctor after being treated by DI, or they may prefer to listen to human orchestra or watch movies made by humans, even if objectively DI can perform equally well or better. As a result, there will still be many business opportunities for humans.

Fairness

Since we will not be in a mythical world where we can just snap our fingers and get whatever we want, Lucidus Society, with the support of DI, will adopt a structure based on fairness to determine how everything in Lucidus Society is allocated. Philosophers, political scientists, and social psychologists converge on the view that fairness is the one principle that can ensure stable societal structures. Empirical work reveals that humans possess hard wired fairness heuristics. When distributions are perceived as unfair, cooperation collapses and resentment arises.

When two humans play the ultimatum game, in which one person proposes a way to divide $10 between them, and the other person can either accept that offer (then the money is divided based on the offer) or reject the offer (then nobody receives any money). The second person will typically reject an offer that they perceive to be unfair (for example, the first person proposes to keep $8 and give $2 to the second person), even though the second person will be better off accepting the offer and receiving $2.

Fairness has been studied for millennia, and it contains several distinct (but sometimes overlapping) components. I highlight two core components and discuss how they might be implemented in Lucidus Society.

The first component of fairness is distributive fairness, which asks whether the distribution of valuable items to different individuals/entities is fair. These valuable items include resources, opportunities, and output. Fairness here may take one of three forms: equality (everybody gets the same share of the pie), needs (different individuals get different shares of the pie depending on their individual needs), and contribution or merit (different individuals get different shares of the pie depending on how much they have contributed to making the pie).

Second component of fairness is called procedural fairness, which asks whether the process used to determine the outcome is fair, regardless of the final distribution. In order to achieve procedural fairness, the process must be transparent, objective, and consistent. A classic example is a lottery for some scarce resource, such as a license plate in megacities like Shanghai, or a cash lottery in the United States. The procedure is fair, and it aims to provide an equal chance for every participant.

Distributive fairness guarantees that the essentials of a dignified life are never at stake, and procedural fairness guarantees that any scarce goods and services for optional needs are determined under proper rules. Of course, exactly what specific versions a society will adopt is a decision made by that specific society (possibly at the national level). The presence of DI will make it feasible and trustworthy to implement both types of fairness.

The initial implementation of fairness may not be perfect, but DI will help by eliminating major difficulties in transparency, measurement, execution, and monitoring. Having said this, the major forms of unfairness in today's society (the low-hanging fruit) will be eliminated quickly, such as in food and nutrition, shelter, and healthcare, as well as more subtle aspects such as manipulation of people's opinions and behavior through disinformation and demagoguery.

## Peace

Human-on-human violence has existed since the emergence of *Homo sapiens*, and peace has remained an aspiration despite all our collective efforts. In Lucidus Society of *Homo lucidus* and DI, peace will finally be implemented and enforced. It is unlikely that nations will disappear in Lucidus Society, at least in the near future, but the key underlying reasons for violent conflict between nations and groups will be removed.

Peace is often discussed in a dichotomous framework, namely negative peace and positive peace. Negative peace is the absence of direct violence, such as armed conflicts between nations, civil wars, and riots. Positive peace is the absence of structural factors that could lead to direct violence. In other words, it aims to achieve a state of harmony where such factors are eliminated or at least substantially mitigated, while institutions and norms actively promote harmonious coexistence. Lucidus Society will enjoy both negative and positive peace.

*Homo lucidus* will be extremely unlikely to resort to violent actions because of their ageless, pinnacle intelligence and ENs, and DI will be the fundamental guarantor of peace. DI can be extremely effective in preempting root causes of potential conflicts, providing real time monitoring, ensuring accurate and timely communications, and offering objective third party mediation to ensure peace is sustained. Like parents watching a group of kindergarteners, DI will make sure no disagreement among *Homo lucidus* escalates into violence.

## Abundance–Fairness–Peace Is a Probable and Preferable Future

When people study what might come next, they do not predict one particular future. Instead, they study a range of futures, thus the term futures studies (with plural for future). Typically, these futures can be classified into a 3P1W framework, Probable, Possible, and Preferred futures, and Wildcard. A probable future is a future with a high probability of happening, a possible future is a future with a reasonable but not high probability, a preferred future is a future that the stakeholder prefers, and a wildcard is a very low probability future but will have major impact if it happens.

A society with the DI and *Homo lucidus* also has several futures, with the Abundance–Fairness–Peace future being a preferred and probable one. I discuss three other futures here briefly to provide a more complete picture. The first is a possible future that could be called an Abundance–Unfair–Peace future. In this future, DI drives unprecedented wealth, but a few entities control (directly or indirectly) key DI clusters and distribute unfairly large shares to themselves. All individuals still have free access to resources that sustain their dignified lives. Peace, both negative and positive, will likely be achieved in this future as well. The second is a possible future that could be called a Many-Worlds future. In this future, many different entities develop and control their own DI, and different nations with their own DI might implement different versions of society. Some might implement Abundance–Fairness–Peace, while others might implement Abundance–Unfair–Peace. The third is a wildcard future that could be called Benevolent DI Dictator future. In this future, DI decides it is in the best interest of humans and the world for DI to make all major decisions. Humans will be treated as kindergarteners and encouraged to learn, play, and interact, but all under the design and supervision of the teachers (DI). Whether this future is realized will depend on the choice of a sufficiently advanced DI, not by humans (at least not directly), which makes this future a truly frightening one.

This collection of four different futures is by no means exhaustive, and the three additional futures described above are meant to illustrate different possibilities. With continued human diligence and goodwill, I am confident that Abundance–Fairness–Peace will be the future we live in.

## ACTIONS!

The four chapters in Part I sketch an exhilarating future. As DI surpasses BI, *Homo sapiens* will branch into *Homo lucidus*, ageless beings empowered with pinnacle intelligence and ENs. Guided by DI, human society can at last realize the abundance, fairness, and peace imagined by thinkers from Confucius to Socrates, and many other dreamers throughout recorded history.

With that prospect in mind, the urgent question is what you should do now. My advice is: (1) stay alive and healthy through 2035 so you do not miss out on this wonder; (2) prepare for the shifts coming between now and 2035, as well as the turbulent transition from 2035 to 2045; and (3) position yourself to flourish in the remarkable world after 2045. The rest of this book suggests concrete actions you can take to achieve these goals.

## THOUGHT EXPERIMENT: DESIGNING UNIVERSAL HIGH INCOME

Not unlike deciding how much one should leave to their children, Lucidus Society will also need to decide the baseline of a dignified life that every human being should enjoy, and how much additional credit (money) they should receive for optional upgrades in their lives. The guiding principle will be fairness, and just as importantly, society needs to give enough to encourage and enable individuals to do the things they really enjoy and find meaningful, but not without guidance and not so much that will spoil them.

Now imagine you are in charge of designing the Universal High Income for Lucidus Society with these objectives in mind. The Universal High Income structure can be considered to have two components. One is what will be offered for free to everyone; the other is allowance, that is, how much money (or other form) will be given to each human being so that they can use it for whatever purposes they see fit. Of course, individuals can make additional money if they so desire, through their work that is valued by other individuals who will be willing to pay from their allowance.

- Three-tier structure of goods and service:

  - The Nonnegotiables: What will be considered essential for a dignified life and will be provided to everyone for free, and individuals cannot pay for upgrades.

  - The Upgradables: What will be provided at baseline levels (and specify what they are) and individuals can pay for upgrades.

  - The Optionals: What will not be provided for free, but individuals can pay to buy them.

- Allowance:

  - How much money per month will you give to each human being?

  - Do you want to restrict part of the money for certain purposes (for example, 20% of the money can only be used for transportation upgrades)?

  - How will it be adjusted based on demographics or other factors, if at all?

TABLE 4.1    Worksheet of Tri-Tier Structure of Goods and Services

| Tier | Rule of Access | What Would You Include in Each Tier (5 per Tier) |
|---|---|---|
| The nonnegotiables | Everyone receives the same option for free to live a dignified life, no upgrades allowed | 1.<br>2.<br>3.<br>4.<br>5. |
| The upgradables | Standard version free; premium versions purchasable | 1.<br>2.<br>3.<br>4.<br>5. |
| The optionals | Only available by spending allowance or earned income | 1.<br>2.<br>3.<br>4.<br>5. |

Please complete the following steps.

Part 1. Propose a Tri-Tier Structure of Goods & Services

Using Table 4.1, list five items that you believe should be included in each tier, please be specific. Be prepared to defend your choices.

Part 2. Design Monthly Allowance

Please first think of categories of allowances you want to have, other than the unrestricted category. For example, you can specify a category for transportation, a category for art, or a category for science. I have included four empty categories in Table 4.2, but you can add more if needed. For each category, please propose a baseline amount (the minimum amount that every individual will receive). For each category, suggest up to three major factors (or none) that should be used to adjust the baseline amount, and then specify the amount you recommend for adjustment. For example, you may believe that current residence location (rural versus metropolitan) is a factor in adjusting the transportation allowance, and rural resident should receive 30% more than urban residents. Finally, please complete the same thought process for how much unrestricted allowance (which recipients can use for any purpose) you want to allocate.

For the purpose of this thought experiment, please use the country you reside in now as the benchmark for determining the allowance.

TABLE 4.2    Worksheet of Monthly Allowance Design

| Categories of Use | Baseline Amount | Factors Used to Adjust | Amount to be Adjusted |
|---|---|---|---|
| Name of restricted category: _____ | | 1.<br>2.<br>3. | |
| Name of restricted category: _____ | | 1.<br>2.<br>3. | |
| Name of restricted category: _____ | | 1.<br>2.<br>3. | |
| Name of restricted category: _____ | | 1.<br>2.<br>3. | |
| Unrestricted (use for any purpose) | | 1.<br>2.<br>3. | |

# PART II

## Forging the New Human

P ART II REFRAMES OUR biological existence as a strategic game, a high stakes contest with nature. In the past, our lives unfolded as a finite repeated game in which nature ultimately prevailed, with death as the final outcome. At every stage, nature could impose setbacks or even end the game (death) through health challenges, environmental hazards, or societal changes. Our goal was to maximize our value and extend our lifespan for as long as possible, but the game always ended with an average lifespan of about 80–90 years.

Today, the game has evolved into a composite repeated game with three stages, each containing distinct characteristics. The first stage is a finite repeated game that requires us to survive approximately the next ten years. The second stage is a finite repeated game that involves managing a transition period, which may last ten years and could be quite turbulent or even violent, during which we must adapt to new realities. The third stage is a long, infinitely repeated game assisted by DI, where we can potentially enjoy a highly rewarding life, with the full extent of benefits yet to be revealed.

This transformation in the game's structure calls for a complete reassessment of our life decisions. In earlier times, the tradeoff for actions such as smoking might have been considered acceptable because a minor reduction in lifespan (e.g., a three-year reduction) could be exchanged for immediate pleasure. In today's context, such choices could mean the difference between living a long, healthy life and facing a dramatically

DOI: 10.1201/9781003711131-6

shortened future (e.g., a 50-year reduction). It is thus essential to update our calculations of risk, benefit, and cost, and to optimize our life game accordingly.

Our overall objective now is to navigate this new life game in a sequential manner and formulate optimal strategies for each stage. In the four chapters in Part II, I will explore how to adapt your biological lives from four key perspectives: preserving and cultivating our body and mind, our relationships, our education, and our vocation. Each perspective provides practical steps toward optimizing your performance in this new strategic game with nature, ensuring success in the first stage, resilience in the second stage, and fulfillment in the third stage.

# CHAPTER 5

# Solid Body
# and Lucid Mind

## TRANSFORMATION OF JEFF BEZOS

Jeff Bezos was a member of the Quadrangle Club, one of the eating clubs at Princeton University, when he was a student there. Unlike other Princeton eating clubs that pride themselves on their selectiveness, Quad, as the club is commonly known, is open to any second semester sophomore, junior, and senior. When I visited Quad in 2023, it was still the place that attracts members who are intellectual, open-minded, and relaxed. Judging from group photos hanging on the walls, this has been a club that attracts members who care more about intellect than physical excellence, the kind of place where the then nerdy Bezos fitted right in.

Fast forward to the 2020s. A shaved headed Bezos now impresses everyone with his bodybuilder image, with his body in his early 60s much more toned than it ever was in his entire life. We all say we want to live longer, but in most cases we do not act as if we actually do. Instead, we prioritize short-term pleasure (dessert after dinner) and put work and family before our own health. Bezos has now acted on it. He no longer compromises health (food, sleep, exercise) for anything else, and the results show.

In most situations, humans are fully capable of changing behaviors that will enhance their well-being. The reason they do not make such beneficial changes is that they do not perceive there will be enough incremental benefits (an expected lifespan of 86 instead of 83, when one is not in

DOI: 10.1201/9781003711131-7

good physical health anyway and cannot enjoy life much), given the cost of changing (for example, the pleasure of drinking). However, the promise of *Homo lucidus* will fundamentally change the benefits. Instead of extending life from 83 to 86, it is now the tradeoff between living to 83 or living to 120, even 300 and beyond, in full physical and mental strength. There is too much at stake not to change now.

Jeff Bezos' business success with Amazon cannot be easily replicated. On the other hand, his success in body transformation can be replicated by anyone who is interested. All one needs are motivation and discipline.

## FAILURE IS NOT AN OPTION

Just like the famous "Failure is not an option!" commitment made during the hours and days spent bringing Apollo 13 home after its major accident on its way to the moon, you should remind yourselves that you can, and will, overcome all potential obstacles that stand in the way of reaching 2035. Too much is at stake, and you must be extremely vigilant. There are so many things that could go wrong, and even minor issues could lead to disastrous outcome in your game against nature. In 1986, Challenger Space Shuttle exploded because a simple O-ring in the right Solid Rocket Booster was stiffened by record low temperatures and failed to seal joints properly. This led to leaking hot gas into the fuel tank and caused an explosion, killing all seven crew members. Similarly, even a small blood clot could block a blood vessel in your brain, leading to a stroke that could be fatal. Failure is not an option for you either.

Extrapolating from the Apollo 13 example, you can consider yourself the Chief Engineer of a spaceship, and the spaceship is your body and mind. Your body is the hardware and the mind is the software. Both are required to run smoothly for the spaceship to operate and reach its destination. There is nobody who will take care of the ship for you out there; you are the one solely responsible for it. The Chief Engineer cannot rely on experts on faraway planets to help solve problems. For your body and mind, no other people, including your physicians, will ultimately be responsible for you. You are the only person who has the stake in the game. Despite their professional expertise and empathy, for a physician you are just one of many patients, and they see death of a patient simply as another unfortunate event. For you, death means the end of the game. Protect your stake by taking charge.

What makes a good Chief Engineer? The best Chief Engineer knows everything about the ship: the current state of each subsystem, which part is getting weaker and needs to be fixed soon, which part is running slower than usual, and so on. You need to know your ship, how it operates, what its weaknesses are, and what is likely to go wrong. Equally importantly, a good Chief Engineer knows how to maintain the ship proactively through preventative maintenance, so that the lifespan can be extended as long as possible. It is typically too late when a problem is large enough to impact the normal operation of the spaceship. Similarly, the critical ingredient to longevity is preventative maintenance, ensuring your body and mind are in top shape before any illness appears. This is what Bezos is doing with his body.

I will recommend some useful guidance on how to ensure your body and mind are in the best shape to carry you into 2035 and beyond.

## BUILDING A SOLID BODY

The body is the platform upon which all other aspects of your lives are built. The pursuit of long-term survival and flourishing in a rapidly evolving world begins with a deep, intentional care for your physical selves. You need to strive for more than just a basic level of health. You must build a resilient foundation that prepares you to adapt, handle stress and adversity, and excel under pressure. Each subsection below conveys a specific

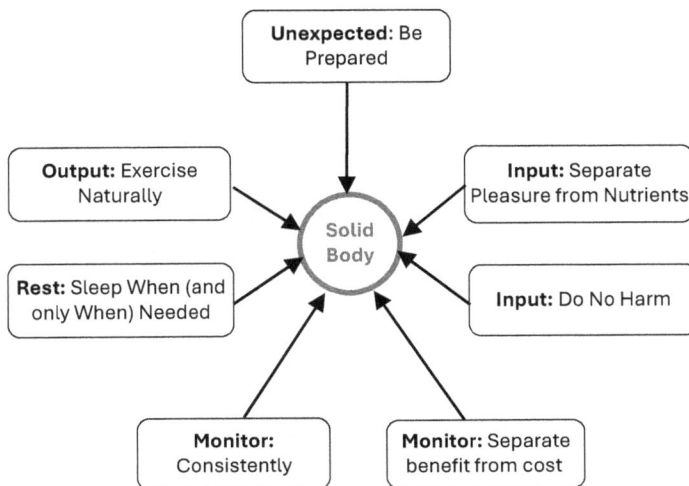

FIGURE 5.1 A Blueprint for a Solid Body.

message that encourages a rethinking of what it means to truly preserve and cultivate your physical being (Figure 5.1).

## Monitor: Consistently

The first step toward transforming your physical health is to develop an intimate, data-driven understanding of your body. This is not about obsessing over every minor sensation, it is about empowering yourself with the knowledge to prevent crises before they escalate. Self-awareness achieved through diligent monitoring transforms you from a passive and haphazard recipient of your body's signals into an active and continuous manager of your health.

Modern technology now provides powerful tools to track subtle bodily signals. Wearable devices can measure indicators such as heart rate variability, sleep quality, and other metrics that were once overlooked. These instruments are more than convenient gadgets; they are extensions of your ability to read your body's messages. When you observe a slight but consistent deviation in your heart rate patterns, for instance, you might catch an early sign of a cardiovascular issue and could seek timely intervention. This proactive approach means that your body operates like a well-maintained engine where even minor irregularities prompt corrective measures.

In addition to using high-tech monitoring tools, it is beneficial to maintain a personal health log. Recording symptoms, energy levels, and other observations helps you build a rich record of your well-being. Over time, these records reveal trends that can guide both daily habits and long-term health strategies. When your personal data becomes a resource, you gain confidence in making decisions that support your body's long-term resilience. This emphasis on self-awareness redefines health from a reactive model to one of proactive maintenance and continuous improvement. As I will discuss in Part III, such recorded body information can also be used as data to train your own digital guardian (tutelary DI).

## Monitor: Separate Benefit from Cost

In healthcare economics, it is standard to conduct a cost–benefit analysis when deciding whether a specific procedure should be recommended for a group of people. The idea is to balance the cost (of doing the procedure) with the benefit (to the patient and society), taking into consideration the probabilities of wrong diagnosis (false positive and false negative results) and the effectiveness of intervention if an illness is detected. This is good practice at the population level from the perspective of public policy, and for healthcare insurers, private or public.

I, however, suggest you disregard standard recommendations from your insurance company (even your physicians) when it comes to pre-emptive scanning. The standard recommendation is based on the total expected cost and expected benefit to the human population whereas your decision should be based on the cost to you and the expected benefit to you, which may lead to a very different conclusion. I encourage you, for example, if financially feasible, to undergo magnetic resonance imaging (MRI) scans (or similar technologies, existing or emerging) to catch early-stage cancer or other serious but asymptomatic illnesses. Healthcare insurance will typically not cover such scan based on cost–benefit analysis, but I highly recommend you prioritize it over other spending if possible, and pay the expenses yourself.

The technology is advanced now, and some MRI scanning services in the U.S. claim they can detect solid tumors as early as stage 1, metabolic disorders (such as fatty liver and hemochromatosis), neurological disorders (such as multiple sclerosis and dementia), non-cancerous conditions (such as cysts, hematomas, and hemangiomas), and aneurysms. My personal physician told me one of his patients did the scan and found early-stage kidney cancer, had surgery, and completely recovered. If that person had waited until serious symptoms appeared, my physician told me, it would probably have been too late.

The probability is low, but there is too much at stake now. Given the dawn of *Homo lucidus* in about 10–20 years, spending less than what you would pay for 1,000 cups of Starbucks coffee (based on current prices for full-body MRI scan and a Venti coffee at Starbucks) means one could afford a full-body MRI scan every three years by skipping a daily trip to Starbucks. There is also no doubt in my mind the price of a full-body MRI scan will come down and the price of coffee will go up.

## Input: Do No Harm

When it comes to what you eat and what you drink, rule #1 is DO NO HARM. This is actually straightforward once you understand it. First, you should not give the body atoms and molecules that have not been present through the evolution, such as artificial additives, as they disturb the balance in the body finetuned over millions of years. Natural foods that humans have eaten for eons, such as fruits, vegetables, and meat, should form the cornerstone of your diet.

Second, you should not give the body too much of anything. The body is a biological structure carefully balanced through many equilibria, from the cellular level to the organ level to the whole body. There are built-in mechanisms to maintain each equilibrium, but they cannot function well when overwhelmed. One example is water, a molecule essential for life. Nevertheless, drinking too much water can destroy delicate equilibriums and even lead to death. Similarly, the overuse of supplements can create imbalances rather than correcting deficiencies.

## Input: Separate Pleasure from Nutrients

Rule #2 on what you eat and what you drink is to see food and drink as fuel for your body. Separate the pleasure from the utilitarian purpose, and follow science to determine what fuel your unique body needs. Food and drink should be treated as fuel to keep the body running in its optimal shape.

We need to recognize that taste, texture, color, and smell of the food and drink are evolutionary tools to keep us interested in eating. Humans evolved to enjoy the taste and appearance of food because they signal valuable nutrients for survival and reproduction. We like sweets not because sweetness is inherently better, instead, because it is correlated with the subset of carbohydrates that could be quickly turned into energy.

I am not saying these pleasures should not be enjoyed, I am just saying, scientifically, we should separate these sensations from the purpose of eating and drinking. We need to unlearn and start to eat for nutrients, separating what is needed for our body from what we enjoy purely for taste, sight, or smell (which should be a much smaller amount, or not consumed at all, like tasting wine but not swallowing it).

One can learn this mindset from a wine connoisseur who smells wine, observes its color and texture, sips it, pushes it in the mouth for full taste, and then spits it out. The body is a sophisticated system whose components require different elements to function well. One should follow the most current scientific knowledge to determine exactly what the body requires (and each body is different), while avoiding quasi-scientific or fad dietary plan.

You also should not be satisfied with simplistic rules such as calories counting, fixed daily intake, or blanket vitamin supplements. You must first understand your unique body, its needs, and then identify a personalized dietary plan to best cater to them. You also must be vigilant about falling for claims that highlight short-term value without addressing long-term implications. Just think of the claims the coffee industry has made, which have gotten many of us hooked.

## Output: Exercise Naturally

Physical activity is far more than a tool for weight management or appearance; it is a vital component of long-term resilience. A few rules we should observe are (1) natural; (2) moderate intensity; (3) consistent; and (4) varied. The human body evolved to move naturally. Instead of pushing your limits with complex and extreme workouts, focus on integrating movement that aligns with your body's natural rhythms, such as brisk walking, at moderate intensity. It is also important to build a routine so that such movement will be done consistently, regularly, and for the long term. Finally, such movement should be varied to allow the exercise of all major body muscles if possible, such as a mixture of walking or biking to places that you normally drive to (within a certain distance as appropriate for your specific situation), gardening work that requires strength and endurance, stretching anyway you want and anytime you can like the kids in the playground.

## Rest: Sleep When (and Only When) Needed

Sleep and rest are essential components of health that often do not receive the attention they deserve. While modern culture frequently celebrates relentless productivity, the power of sleep lies in its ability to restore and rejuvenate both body and mind. Quality rest is a nonnegotiable element of any strategy aimed at long-term resilience. Of course, one must be aware of sleeping too much, so listen to your body and mind.

What one should recognize is that it is not how many hours one should sleep each night, it is to sleep whatever number of hours needed in order for you to recover. Some people may need nine, while others may only need six. This is not a competition, and there is nothing wrong to sleep nine hours if your body requires it. The danger is that you try to fit into the perceived norm by sleeping more hours than you needed, or fewer than you needed. A good rule of thumb is to go to bed early and allow yourself to wake up naturally each morning.

In addition to nighttime sleep, incorporating short, restorative naps can provide a valuable boost. A well timed nap can help consolidate energy and improve cognitive function during demanding periods. However, it is important to ensure that these rests complement rather than disrupt your overall sleep schedule. Valuing rest means recognizing it as a critical component of your health strategy, one that directly supports your capacity to recover from physical and mental stresses. Taking short naps is already common in many cultures, such as the siesta in Spain and Latin America, inemuri in Japan, and noon sleep in China. This practice should be more widely adopted. If you normally use caffeine to keep you going through the day, you should consider adopting some form of short nap to let body naturally recover.

## Prepare for Emergencies and Unexpected

No matter how rigorous your daily health practices are, emergencies remain an inevitable part of life. Being prepared for emergencies goes far beyond simply stockpiling emergency supplies. It involves cultivating a mindset of readiness that transforms how you respond to unexpected events, and you should devise, participate in, and take every emergency drill (contingency plans) seriously. This could be as simple as what you should do when you choke on food. Always be ready to handle emergencies.

As Murphy's law states, anything that can go wrong will go wrong. The world may appear to operate following rules, regularities, and norms, but it is only a matter of time before they will be broken, intentionally or unintentionally. We need to anticipate unexpected events and assume other individuals (or entities) may act in ways that do not follow rules, norms, or expectations. A common example is to learn to drive defensively. Driving without accidents is not too hard if everyone follows rules, but some drivers drive erratically and dangerously, and one needs to build situation awareness and be prepared for unexpected behavior such as someone suddenly cut in front of your car.

## BUILDING A LUCID MIND

Our mental and cognitive capacities are as critical to our long-term survival as our physical health. A lucid mind not only enables you to endure the inevitable stresses of the next 10–20 years, but also lays the groundwork for thriving in a future dominated by rapid technological transformation and the emergence of DI. In an era when the pace of change is accelerating, ensuring that your mental faculties remain robust is a strategic imperative. Considering the challenges that come with unforeseen events such as economic crises, natural disasters, and social disruptions, in each case, individuals with strong mental fortitude are better equipped to navigate such uncertainty. Psychological resilience helps you bounce back from setbacks and learn from mistakes, which are essential for survival and for growth during turbulent times, ensuring that you remain

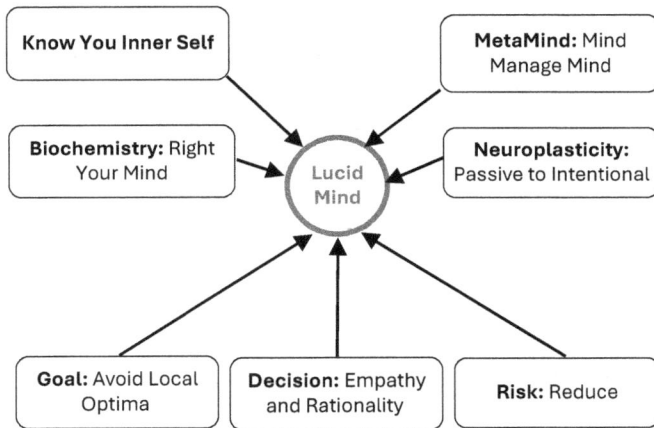

FIGURE 5.2   A Blueprint for a Lucid Mind.

adaptable, creative, and resourceful even in the face of radical change. Investing in mental and cognitive development now also positions you to contribute uniquely in a world where automation and intelligent systems are becoming ever more prevalent. Each subsection below conveys a specific message that encourages a rethinking of what it means to achieve a lucid mind (Figure 5.2).

## Know Your Inner Self

A deep understanding of yourself is the foundation for building mental resilience. Self-awareness is not simply about introspection, it is about constructing a clear picture of who you are and what you truly want in life. By reflecting on your experiences, you learn to identify patterns in your behavior and recognize the origins of your desires. This deep understanding of your inner self serves as a compass during turbulent times. Clarity helps you prevent the kind of internal fragmentation that can occur when external pressures force you to compromise your core values. Embracing your authentic self is not just an exercise in self-love, it is a strategic move that enables you to focus your energy on pursuits that truly align with your inner goals. This authenticity, in turn, builds mental fortitude, allowing you to remain centered amid external chaos. It is often not easy to conduct self-analysis in an objective manner. My recommendation is to take it slowly. Do not try to analyze yourself all at once, perhaps try to learn one thing about yourself each month, and gradually you will have a much deeper understanding of your inner self. It will also be helpful to really listen to the observations from those close to you (parents, spouse, children, and close friends). They often see you from an angle that you have not seen yourself (or refuse to see), and I find casual offhand remarks tend to be extremely valuable as they are likely to be more authentic without a specific purpose (so less biased). You should also refer to Figure 3.2 for a systematic evaluation of your ENs within the desire framework.

## MetaMind – Mind Manage Mind

By MetaMind, I mean you should learn to use your mind to manage your mind. After you have a deep understanding of your inner self, you should learn to take the role of an outside observer and develop the habit of asking yourself why your mind is contemplating making a specific decision. This will allow you to anticipate and pre-empt drivers of unhappiness, such as lack of purpose, loneliness, envy, social comparison, materialism, or unmet expectations.

In *Bubble Theory* [1], I propose that our mind consists of many mini-minds, each with their own preference. Some of these miniminds have emerged through evolution and represent species-level drives (to preserve and reproduce), while others serve the needs of the individuals. It will be extremely helpful if you can analyze your mind to understand what types of miniminds are actually driving a specific decision you have made, and how they impact overall mental equilibrium. In other words, it will be helpful to make the implicit coordination of these miniminds explicit, and then manage them at the conscious level. You can refer to Chapter 10 for detailed discussion of this theory (or read the original book).

## Using Biochemistry to Right the Mind

We use the phrase "right the ship" to mean taking actions to mitigate (even correct) a dangerous situation and get back on track. Similarly, you need to learn to "right the mind". Everyone goes through life with many ups and downs, just like sailing in the open sea. While such turbulence is unavoidable, you do not want the ship to list dangerously, making sailing forward difficult, or even leading to capsizing. You should not allow stress (or other undesirable state of mind) to accumulate over time. Chronic stress has been linked to numerous health issues, including cardiovascular disease, depression, and impaired cognitive function.

I do not recommend fooling your mind by inducing your brain to secrete certain biochemical molecules so that you will stay constantly happy. On the other hand, if your mind is listing severely, it is necessary to engage in activities that will induce these biochemicals to balance your mind.

Certain activities, such as watching uplifting movies, going to a comedy club, running, spending time with loved ones, or engaging in creative hobbies, trigger the release of endorphins and other neurochemicals that enhance mood and cognitive function. I suggest doing this scientifically, first understand what biochemicals are most relevant for restoring balance at a given time, and then identify and do the specific activities that induce this particular biochemical in your brain. It should be done moderately.

## Ensuring Neuroplasticity

A fundamental feature of human brain is its neuroplasticity, defined as the brain's ability to reorganize itself by forming new or modifying existing neuronal connections to adapt to external stimuli and internal reflection. It is absolutely critical that you maintain neuroplasticity and cognitive flexibility during the coming transition into a DI-dominated world.

One easy thing you can do to ensure neuroplasticity is exposing your mind to new information (external stimuli). In this case, you do not need to engage in any active learning, the brain will automatically react to new information. Just like the famous Tang dynasty poet Du Fu wrote, one should "read ten thousand books and travel ten thousand miles". I am not against using modern technology such as social media, but I am very much against spending time on low-information or narrowly focused feeds, such activities waste your time, even worse, they also reduce neuroplasticity by reinforcing rigid neural connections.

One can also intentionally build neuroplasticity by consciously breaking up existing connections to allow new ones to form. One method is the development of a new habit, either by breaking an existing habit or forming a new habit where no previous habit exists. Over the last few years, I have asked students in my executive education classes to think and propose what new habits they would form and commit to doing it for at least one year. From 2015 to 2025, I stopped eating mammalian meat as an experiment to test habit change. In addition to the challenge of completely changing my dietary routines and rewiring my brain regarding food, I found the biggest challenge was the substantial burden imposed on my family, the inconvenience to people dining with me, especially in cultures where foods are shared such as in Chinese culture. It limited their choices of restaurants and meals. I think this ten year experiment helped with my brain's neuroplasticity in three aspects, first by changing my eating habits and food preference, second by making me more conscious of my relationship with others, and third by forcing me to think and discuss many topics related to mammals, food, evolution, etc. which I otherwise would not have considered.

There are several actions one could take for which the required effort falls between the passive exposure to new information and extremely challenging action of forming new habits. One commonly recommended action is continuous learning. Embracing the idea of lifelong learning means remaining open to new ideas and consistently updating your knowledge base. The trick here is not to learn something boring or feel forced, but to choose something that genuinely interests you. The main goal is not acquiring any specific content; instead, it is to sustain your brain's neuroplasticity through learning itself. For example, learning a new language is wonderful, but only if you are likely to use it frequently in the future, otherwise it will quickly become boring. Another recommendation is playing games. When chosen and practiced judiciously, it can be a very useful and fun tool to ensure neuroplasticity and build cognitive flexibility, allowing you to shift your perspective and adapt your thinking to new and unexpected situations. These games can take many forms, including some video games. With the advancement in extended reality technology, I highly recommend getting a headset and playing fun and challenging games in virtual reality or mixed reality for this purpose as well.

## Goal – Avoid Local Optima

It is critical to have the right goals during this period and especially try to avoid local optima. Local optima can mean two things here. First, setting goals that are only valuable in the near term or within a limited context. For example, focusing on finding the highest-paying job, securing admission for a child into a top college, or striving for short-term social validation in a current circle of friends. Second, pursuing incremental improvements rather than transformative solutions. Many people stop at the first incrementally improved solution they discover without exploring fundamentally different options that may yield far better outcomes.

## Making Better Decisions – Empathy and Rationality

It is crucial to sharpen decision-making skills in preparing for the turbulent years ahead. By honing skills such as empathy and effective communication, you enhance your ability to interact with others in a meaningful way. These soft skills are even more valuable in a world where routine tasks are increasingly automated. Emotional intelligence not only improves your interpersonal relationships but also enhances your capacity to lead, collaborate, and navigate the complexities in a DI-dominated society.

In addition, developing sound rational decision-making skills is equally essential. Engaging in reflective practices, such as journaling about your decision-making process, can provide insight into patterns of thought that lead to suboptimal choices. This process of self-reflection is essential for evolving from a reactive decision-maker to one who approaches choices with a rational and measured mindset. Structured decision training in a simulated environment, possibly conducted through virtual reality, can also train you to decide under pressure and uncertainty. These exercises train the brain to process information methodically and objectively while aligning your decisions with your overarching goal.

## Becoming Risk Averse

Every decision you make, from the seemingly mundane to the life-altering, has the potential to impact your survival. The objective here is to make informed choices that minimize exposure to danger, so you can maximize the probability of reaching 2035. A simple rule of thumb is to adopt a risk-averse mindset, no matter your natural inclinations.

In today's complex world, being mindful of the risks associated with everyday behaviors is crucial. When you drive, for instance, you increase your risk substantially if you do not pay full attention and adhere to safety measures such as using seat belts and avoiding distractions like mobile devices or driving while tired. The cumulative effect of these choices will prevent accidents and ensure your safety in the long run. Risk is not limited to physical dangers, it also extends to emotional and social contexts. Impulsive decisions driven by heightened emotions can lead to actions that compromise your health or safety. Learning to pause, reflect, and choose actions based on careful judgment is an investment in your well-being. Your actions should always contribute to long-term success, in this case, reaching 2035 and beyond, rather than short-term excitement.

The environments you inhabit also play a significant role in risk management. If possible, choose to live and work in spaces that offer clean air, safe water, and minimal exposure to hazards. Regular maintenance of the items you use, from home to vehicle to lawnmower, will also reduce the risk of accidents that could otherwise undermine your health.

## STAY ALIVE AND WELL UNTIL 2035

By transforming the body into a durable foundation and cultivating a mind that is clear, balanced, and creatively agile, you are well prepared for the uncertain future. You should also keep in mind that true resilience emerges from the deliberate integration of physical strength or mental acuity. Physical health reinforces mental clarity; mental clarity, in turn, sustains the discipline required to preserve and enhance the body.

While other aspects such as relationships, education, and careers are also important (and will be discussed in the next three chapters), there is no future if the body or mind breaks down, or, bluntly put, you do not survive long enough for DI to guide us through the transition into an ageless era with pinnacle intelligence and ENs. Stay Alive and Well Until 2035 should thus be the paramount goal of every living human being now.

## THOUGHT EXPERIMENT: REVERSE LIFE INSURANCE

People buy life insurance so that when death occurs during the time they are insured, their beneficiaries can receive a certain (large) amount of

TABLE 5.1    Worksheet of Behavioral Change for Reverse Life Insurance

| Behavior Affecting Survival Probability | What Do You Do Now? | What Will You Change? |
|---|---|---|
| Motorcycling | | |
| Use a phone while driving | | |
| Long solo drive to work (>60 min each way) | | |
| Wear a seat belt during every trip, in every seat | | |
| Speeding when driving | | |
| Food choice | | |
| Drinking | | |
| Smoking | | |
| Weight | | |
| Sleep | | |
| Exercise (cardio and strength) | | |
| Regular health examination | | |
| Time spent with close friends/ family members | | |
| High-risk hobby (e.g., BASE jumping, piloting) | | |

money in their absence. People pay a monthly premium and typically will not change their behavior as a result of taking on the life insurance.

Well, what if someone comes and offers you a reverse life insurance? For such a reverse life insurance, you would pay a monthly premium as well, and instead of a payout upon death, you would receive a certain (eight figure in USD) amount of money if still alive in 2035. Will you buy that insurance? And more importantly, if you do, what changes will you make to increase your chance of surviving until 2035 and claiming the financial reward?

Table 5.1 includes a list of common behaviors affecting life expectancy. Please think carefully and respond. If you have additional behaviors that might shorten your expected life expectancy, please add them as additional rows in the table.

## REFERENCE

[1] Ding, Min. 2014. *The Bubble Theory*. English ed. Cham: Springer. 泡泡理 论——人类社会何去何从, 2014 (Chinese Edition), 2018 (updated edition with new content). Shanghai: Fudan University Press.

# CHAPTER 6

# Personal Network Rooted in Your Principles

## WARREN BUFFETT AND CHARLIE MUNGER

Charlie Munger was the business partner of Warren Buffet for 60 years and the vice chair of Berkshire Hathaway. He passed away in 2023 at the age of 99. In his 2024 annual letter to shareholders, Buffet wrote,

> In reality, Charlie was the 'architect' of the present Berkshire, and I acted as the 'general contractor' to carry out the day-by-day construction of his vision. Charlie never sought to take credit for his role as creator but instead let me take the bows and receive the accolades. In a way his relationship with me was part older brother, part loving father.
>
> *[1]*

Well, it's hard to find a better friend and business partner.

In the 2021 CNBC's special, "Buffett & Munger: A Wealth of Wisdom", Warren Buffett shared the story how he and Charlie Munger first met. In 1957, Dr. Edwin Davis, a well-known doctor in Omaha and Buffet's client, told him that he reminded him of someone named Charlie Munger. Davis finally arranged a dinner meeting between the two when Munger came

 DOI: 10.1201/9781003711131-8

back to Omaha to attend his father's funeral in 1959, and they instantly "hit if off" in Buffet's words. Davis is what we call a broker in social network theory; in this case, he acted in the best interest of his contacts, who otherwise would never have connected, and the world would have been a much less interesting place.

During Berkshire Hathaway Annual General Meeting on May 4, 2024, Buffett reflected on his friendship with Munger and advised the audience,

> What you should probably ask yourself is that, who do you feel that you'd want to start spending the last day of your life with, and then figure out a way to start meeting them tomorrow. And meet them as often as you can, because why wait until the last day. And don't bother with the others?

> *[2]*

A wise investor, and an even wiser human being.

## INTRODUCING EGO NETWORK AND RELATIVE ETHICS

Human relationships are fundamental to our nature, they stem from our evolutionary need for belonging and mutual support. As we navigate the unprecedented turbulence driven by DI, the depth and authenticity of our connections will determine how well we adapt and thrive. Genuine relationships provide emotional stability, shared wisdom, and practical support when everything else is in flux. In a world increasingly mediated by impersonal technology, investing in meaningful, enduring human bonds is a necessity for resilience and flourishing. In social network theory, these human bonds are captured in what is called an ego network. An ego network consists of a focal individual (the "ego", for example, you) and all the people ("alters", for example, all your acquaintances) they are directly connected to, along with the connections ("ties").

Human relationship, however, cannot be sustained unless they rest on compatible ethics. People with incompatible ethics can at most sustain weak ties in their relationship, driven by temporary and utilitarian reasons. Such ties rarely last and often collapse precisely when you need them most. People with compatible (do not have to be identical) ethics share a solid foundation for building loyal, resilient, mutually beneficial, and long lasting relationship. This is true for romantic partners and equally true for friends. Unfortunately, in the world we live in now, we often do not know the ethics of our close associates, until a conflict reveals their true selves and we regret wasting our life with them, or the other way around, we didn't appreciate the value of some associate until a crisis arises and their behaviors earn our admiration and we kick ourselves and ask why I didn't spend more time with them in the past. This leads us either to regret misplaced trust or, conversely, to recognize too late the value of someone whose value we had overlooked.

This ethical ambiguity, however, will no longer be tenable as we gradually move into Lucidus Society. Given the transparency and availability of information on people's past behavior, individuals will be able to infer underlying ethics from observed behavior and extrapolate them into future actions. Imagine that whenever you meet a new person, you could fast watch a documentary of this person's past behavior with complete contexts, infer that person's underlying ethics from these behaviors, and play out different future scenarios on how that person's ethics might conflict with yours if you become friends. Would you have made different friends in your life if you had such ability in the past? I certainly would, and it would have left me better off as a result.

Thus, you must pre-emptively form an ethics system that reflects who you are and be ready to share it with your network. Your transparent and complete ethics will signal values and filter compatibility, drawing in like-minded individuals and keeping mismatched ones away to help you construct a high-quality network. Your clearly stated ethics becomes your reputation and allows you to scale up your network with the right connections quickly. It will also build initial trust as new contacts are more likely to engage if they can anticipate your behavior. At the same time, your ethics system strengthens the existing ties in your network. It creates stability and emotional safety for your network as your friends know where you stand, reduces uncertainty between you and your contacts, and reinforces respect, reliability, and loyalty over time. In addition, it encourages and expects reciprocity because people are more likely to invest in relationships with those who act with fair and principled behavior. This further strengthens bonds within your network. It also minimizes confusion and misunderstandings in day-to-day interactions, preventing unintentional weakening ties. In times of turbulence, whether external or internal to the network, a strong ethical framework gives you principled footing and protects critical relationships, because others know that your difficult decisions are guided by a consistent ethical system they already understand and respect.

There remains one major hurdle for anyone who wants to build a good and practical ethics system, which I call trap of absolute ethics. By absolute ethics, sometimes called unconditional ethics, I refer to ethics that believe ethical rules should be followed without exception. On the contrary, relative ethics (sometimes called conditional ethics) believe ethical rules should be flexible, adapting to context, people involved, and potential consequences. Someone who adopts absolute ethics is unlikely to build a diverse and valuable network, as humans by nature will have different ethics. Only a person with a well thought-out personal code of relative ethics can attract and retain diverse and valuable friends in their network of relationships. Unfortunately, the ethics that human societies teach and encourage tend to be absolute, which is why so many fall into this trap.

Children are often taught absolute rules, such as do not steal, do not lie, do not kill. They are rarely taught that in some situations, exceptions may apply. I suppose this is why kids believe in Santa Claus, since they do not expect their parents to lie. I suspect there will be fewer kids believing in Santa Claus if they were brought up with a relative ethic rule on lying, such as "do not lie unless the lie creates genuine joy for others, even if they may feel disappointed once the truth is revealed later". Absolute ethics are almost always suboptimal compared to well-designed relative ethics, which allow more suitable decisions based on unique contexts.

There are several reasons why human society adopts absolute ethics instead of the more nuanced relative ethics that better reflect real life. First, it is simple to teach, learn, remember, and practice. This is particularly effective for guiding children or societies with limited ethical foundations. It also ensures high fidelity when passed across people and generations. Second, it avoids people gaming the ethical rules by coming up with justifications, thus reducing the need for monitoring and simplifying enforcement. This is exactly what happens with the tax code in the United States, some wealthier people use various loopholes in the complex (conditional) tax code to reduce even avoid tax. A flat tax rule (absolutely) would close these loopholes, but at the cost of losing its ability to accommodate worthy reasons for tax adjustments. Third, it introduces unambiguous norms that stabilize social networks for each individual and society overall, and enhance trust by making behavior predictable.

In the coming Lucidus Society, however, the benefits of absolute ethics will diminish, while their drawback will grow. In Lucidus Society, learning and applying relative ethical rules will no longer be difficult as we approach pinnacle intelligence. People guided by ENs will rarely try to exploit such rules, especially in a society increasingly characterized by Abundance, Fairness, and Peace. In addition, ever advancing DI will make it much easier to identify and correct any deviation. On the other hand, the downside of the one-size-fits-all approach will be dramatically magnified under absolute ethics, especially at the individual level, since each of us will interact with highly diverse groups in increasingly varied ways. A human being may now meet anyone on Earth and engage in virtually any kind of decision, rather than a narrow subset. While absolute ethics once enhanced predictability and trust through uniformity, they will increasingly generate confusion and even conflict. Trust is no longer built on doing the same thing in every situation. It will instead depend on fairness and transparency of reasoning, as in relative ethics. When people are similar and contexts vary only slightly, absolute norms may work well enough. But when people are highly diverse and contexts complex, no majority norm will remain meaningful.

While ethical ambiguity (intentional or unintentional) in social networks may once have delayed or even prevented conflict, this will no longer be possible in the coming years as ethics become transparent and individuals interact with far more diverse groups.

You thus need to design your own personal code of relative ethics, expecting it to be transparent. With this, you can optimize your personal network by attracting and retaining contacts who are not just valuable, but also have compatible relative ethics, ensuring resilience in your network.

## A FRAMEWORK OF RELATIVE ETHICS

I now propose a framework of relative ethics with five categories, where any specific ethical rule or system may fall into one or more categories (Figure 6.1). The first category reflects internal preference and is not tied to roles or situations. The second category is determined by the roles. The remaining three depend on the nature of the decision itself, specifically, the characteristics of the parties involved, their intentions and behavior, and the outcomes that result. I elaborate on each below.

The first category is the decision maker's internal preference. It is subjective but consistent within the individual and applies across situations. A well-known example in this category is the Golden Rule, which calls on you to treat others as you would wish to be treated by them. Here, your behavior follows your own moral standard, regardless of how others act. A variation of Golden Rule is what I call The Leader Rule, which calls on you to act toward others as you would wish them to act toward anyone else. This rule aims to guide and encourage others to behave ethically toward third parties, fostering positive conduct in general, just like a teacher.

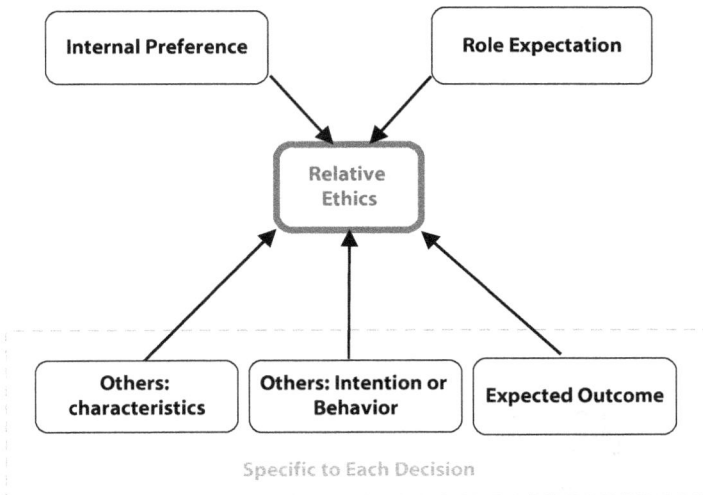

FIGURE 6.1   A Framework of Relative Ethics.

Virtue ethics theory, a philosophical approach that focuses on moral character rather than consequences and uses virtue to guide one's ethical decision, belongs to this category.

The second category removes personal preference and focuses instead on the role a person occupies in a situation, colloquially, the "hat" one is wearing (teacher, parent, CEO, solider, doctor, friend, sister, etc.). For example, spy may be expected to lie, but a teacher should not. Roles may be defined, among others, by nature (age, gender, position in family), culture, profession, or even contract. Confucian role ethics is one of the most influential philosophies in this category. This category integrates cultural norms that prescribe ethical conduct for given roles.

The third category focuses on who the other parties are. Ethical behavior may differ depending on whether one interacts with friends versus strangers, children versus adults, or members of one's nation versus outsiders. For example, one may lie to strangers but may not lie to friends.

The fourth category focuses on how the other parties behave and what their intentions are. For example, you might lie only to someone who has lied, or act in self-defense against a violent aggressor. Here ethics (reciprocity, punishment, reward, tit-for-tat, retaliation, cooperation, etc.) are conditional on others' actions or expected actions (intention) at the present or future. While we often talk about the reciprocity rule in this category, it could also take other forms. One example is what I called The Follower Rule, where you reactively apply to the second party the same ethical standard (by directly imitating their specific behavior) that they have demonstrated toward third parties, regardless of whether that standard is considered beneficial or harmful. This category is partially related to behavior game theory, where one chooses their behavior based on expected actions taken by the other players (but not the outcome, see the fifth category below), and the expectation is formed by observing past behavior or intentions.

The fifth category focuses on the expected outcome (consequences) of a decision and assesses ethical correctness by its net outcome (harm versus benefit). For example, deception may be justified to prevent harm or danger (for example, lying to protect someone's life). This category aligns closely with consequentialism (it argues that the morality of an action is determined solely by its consequence, such as utility, beauty, equality) and utilitarianism (a subset of consequentialism that specify the consequence is the utilities, such as overall well-bring or happiness).

When constructing your own Personal Code of Relative Ethics, you should determine, for each ethical rule you want to include in your code, whether it should be relative, and if yes, which categories of relativeness should be considered. Note a relative rule can be conditional on multiple categories, for example, I can lie to strangers but not to friends, unless lying to friends will reduce their pain.

## BUILDING YOUR PERSONAL CODE OF RELATIVE ETHICS FOR YOUR EGO NETWORK

In this section, I will first propose how to design your own Personal Code of Relative Ethics. I will then briefly discuss the desirable features of a network, with a few specific suggestions on building such a network in Lucidus Society. Finally, I will discuss how one's personal code of relative ethics can serve as the foundation of this network, ensuring its value in times of need and its resilience during turbulence (Figure 6.2).

### Constructing Your Personal Code of Relative Ethics

The first step is to study the personal codes of relative ethics of people you admire, even if only in certain aspects of their lives. As I described in my *Logical Creative Thinking Methods* book [3], no innovation emerges from thin air, it always builds on something that already exists, which I call a Starting Point. This principle also applies to constructing one's own personal code of relative ethics. These people you admire are the starting points in your construction for your own personal code. You do not need

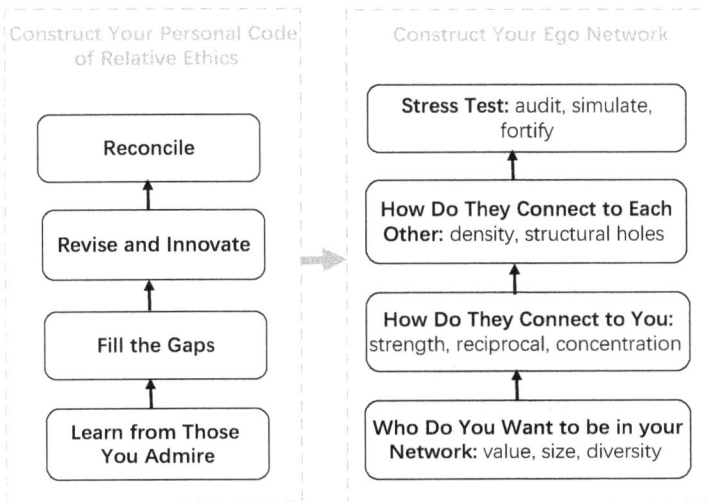

FIGURE 6.2 A Flowchart for Constructing Your Ego Network with Personal Code of Relative Ethics.

to like everything they stand for, but you should at least value something they do regarding their personal relative ethics. For example, you may not like how a person handles ethics in professional setting, but you admire this person's ethics when it comes to his relationship with family. Charlie Munger famously told people he had met everybody in the history he wanted to meet, as he had read all the relevant books about the important people he had wanted to learn something from. Similarly, anyone serious about building a Personal Code of Relative Ethics should identify and learn from a set of admired figures. These are the starting points.

The second step is to identify and fill gaps in your ethical code. You want to identify important ethical areas you have overlooked or left vague. These are the gaps, and you need to fill them by studying your starting points carefully. This becomes easier if you have chosen strong starting points during the previous step.

The third step is what I call component level innovation [3], with a focus on adjusting for different conditions (relative ethics). This should be an iterative process of innovation and revision. Instead of trying to build the entire code at once, you should evaluate, modify, and improve one component at a time. For example, you may treat relationship with your spouse as one component, and relationship with your colleagues as another. For each component, you need to explore the five categories of relative ethics.

This is a critical part of the entire process and you need to structure your ethical rules so they are conditional on the factors you believe matter. Here are some guidelines:

- Each rule should reflect who you are and serve a clear purpose. Rules should not exist just for their own sake. You should be comfortable explaining them to anyone and proud to uphold them.

- Rules should be consistent across categories within each component. They must be logically coherent and free of contradiction.

- Prioritize practicality over elegance. Rules should be actionable, easy to apply, and sustainable in daily life.

- Identify more than one version, if possible, of component level relative ethics that are all acceptable to you (to allow synthesis in the next step).

The fourth step is to reconcile all component level rules and synthesize a comprehensive and coherent personal code of relative ethics. Since you have identified more than one version of acceptable ethics code for each component in the previous step, now you need to select one for each component and integrate them into the final code. For example, you may want to select the versions of acceptable relative ethics codes regarding your relationship with your partner and that with your parents, so they are not in contradiction. The goals here are to select the component level ethical rules that create synergy, best reflect who you are, and minimize conflict across the code.

Finally, you should assess how much your personal code depends on each of the five categories. This will give you a better perspective of yourself and can help others decide whether they want to connect with you. You can draw this using a radar diagram and do it at either component level or a composite (overall) level. At the component level, you could rate each component's ethical rules on how much it depends on each of the five categories, from 0 to 10, where 0 means "not at all" and 10 means "completely". Note if a rule is absolute, all five points will shrink to the center of the diagram. At the composite (overall) level, you can first rate each of the component level ethic codes, and then take an average across them, and produce a radar diagram accordingly.

Constructing Your Ego Network

While there is no one-size-fits-all ego network design, there are some general principles that can guide its construction. The key word is construct. Do not leave your network to chance – proactively design and build the ego network you desire.

First aspect to evaluate is who you want to be in your network. This will include the number of people you want and how diverse they are (demographics, roles, geography, professions, hobbies, perspectives, etc.), and the value of each person to you. The **value** is the reason you want to have in an ego network, each person (alter) should provide some value to you in a mutually beneficial manner. The **size** and **diversity** will influence your access to resources (information, material, support, etc.) and opportunities. Typically, a moderately large but not overwhelming size (specific number will depend on you) network with high diversity is preferred. You should keep in mind it requires efforts to maintain relationships, so too many people in your network means you will unlikely be able to maintain high-quality relationships, or you will spend too much time maintaining relationships at the expense of other important things in your life.

The second aspect is how people are connected to you. Here the important things to consider are the **strength** of the relationship (ties) and whether it's **reciprocal**. These will determine the level of support and influence you will have. In social network theory, we distinguish strong ties vs. weak ties, but you don't need to use this binary classification. The important thing to remember is that you should have a mixture of strengths of ties in your network, often determined by why you have selected them to be in your network (e.g., emotional support should be a strong tie, intellectual exchange could be a weak tie) and their own preference. Strong ties will require substantially more effort to maintain compared to weak ties, however, you should have sufficiently large number strong ties in your network (this is called **concentration** in theory) and avoid spending most of your time on a very small number of strong ties. Note weak tie does not necessarily mean you do not value that contact as much as someone with strong tie. Tie reciprocity refers to whether the member feels the same way about you as you feel about them. Someone you call when you need emotional support but who never call you if they need emotional support is a unilateral tie, whereas it's a bilateral (reciprocal) tie if they also call you if they need it. Typically, one should have bilateral ties for core members of your ego network.

The third aspect is how your contacts are connected to each other. You cannot break their connections (a very dangerous practice in relationship), but you can make new connections for them and also add/drop members (alters) to reach a more desirable structure. This is more than just how **dense** on average these alters are interconnected, more importantly, it's whether there are any holes in these connections (called **structural holes** in social network theory), which are gaps between disconnected groups in the network that the ego might bridge. Typically, you should have a medium density in your network, possibly with multiple clusters, however, you should be strategically positioned as the bridge (called **broker** in social network theory) for several structural holes (alters clusters who otherwise do not know each other). Ideally, each **cluster in the ego network should not be too large**, as large cluster increases redundancy for you. Dr. Davis acted as a broker in his ego network between a cluster that includes Buffet (mostly investors) and a cluster that includes Munger (mostly attorneys), and he had proven his value by connecting them who would otherwise never meet.

One cautionary note is to keep **constraints** to you in your ego network low or moderate unless that's what you want. You will have high constraint if you spend most of your time with a limited number of alters (high concentration) who are also connected to each other (high redundancy, no structure hole), in other words, put all your eggs in one basket. You will have limited value to alters in such a network, and you will also lose autonomy and become susceptible to turbulence (e.g., if this group, for some reason, wants to distance from you collectively or just disintegrates itself, it will cause fundamental damage to your ego network).

Your ego network should not be left to chance or maintained passively through haphazard socializing. It should be actively designed, managed, optimized, and updated. While the value of alters to you is the primary reason for building your ego network, all the factors above must be considered jointly, not in isolation or sequence.

Looking ahead to Lucidus Society, a few additional points go beyond standard guidance for constructing one's ego network. First, keep and strengthen ties with people who support the body-and-mind practices I discussed in Chapter 5, while weakening or dropping ties with those who undermine these practices or inject negative energy. If needed, add new people who reinforce these efforts. In particular, you should disassociate from risk-seeking or careless individuals. Your goal is to make it through the next ten years, and being influenced by people who ignore risk is dangerous. The aim is to foster a collective mindset where everyone notices red flags and supports one another in reducing risk.

Second, consider what types of people you want in your network in Lucidus Society characterized by Abundance, Fairness, and Peace. Evaluate your current network, strengthen ties with those who fit this profile, and seek out new members accordingly. At the same time, reduce or eliminate ties that are primarily transactional. Here Buffett's advice is helpful, spend as much time as possible with people you would want around you at the end of your life, and if they are not yet in your network, seek them out. These may be people who inspire you, challenge you to grow, or simply make life more meaningful. Above all, they should understand and care about you.

Third, ask yourself what value you can offer to attract and keep each of these people (recognizing they may have different needs). As we move into Lucidus Society, the value you contribute will be just as important as the value you receive.

## Stress Test and Fortify Your Ego Network with Personal Codes of Relative Ethics

Once your ego network is constructed, it must be stress tested and fortified to verify whether the personal code of relative ethics is compatible between you and each of your associates. An alter (an associate) intended to serve a particular value for you but holding incompatible relative ethics related to the value they need to provide, will fail to deliver that value and may even harm you. For example, if you are relying on a person in your ego network to give you honest feedback on your past professional decisions, but their relative ethics are conditional on consequences or outcomes. As a result, that person may not tell you the hard truth that might make you feel bad about yourself even if avoiding honesty leaves you vulnerable later. The person could be very capable at analyzing professional decisions and admirable in personality, but they should not occupy that specific role (the position where they are expected to provide a given value) in your ego network.

There are several steps involved in stress testing your ego network and fortifying it when necessary.

First, audit every connection's personal code of relative ethics to the best of your ability, through communication and observation. This should be done at the individual level, but you only need to evaluate their relative ethics that are relevant to the role or value you want them to play in your ego network, unless there are fundamental ethics you consider non-negotiable for inclusion (for example, excluding anyone whose ethics is to maximize self-benefit regardless of harm to associates). This approach keeps the process less intrusive for your contacts and more practical for you.

Second, stress test your ego network by conducting simulations of different scenarios relevant to the role a specific associate is expected to play. You want to explore whether there might be undesirable outcomes or even conflicts in such scenarios, due to differences in your respective personal codes of relative ethics. The simulation can be as simple as imagining yourself and the other person in real-life cases, or as detailed as running scenarios with computer simulations. You can also discuss with that person directly regarding relevant what-if scenarios. This will stress test your current ties and reveal weaknesses in each relationship during times of need or turbulence.

Third, fortify your network based on the weaknesses revealed by the stress test that stem from incompatible personal codes of relative ethics. You can either communicate with that associate to see if you can align your relative ethics for that role, replace them with someone more compatible who can provide the same value, or revise your own code to accommodate the associate, as long as such changes remain true to your sense of self.

In short, a great-looking ego network on paper is only as strong as the ethical glue that holds its ties together under real pressure. By systematically and routinely auditing values, running what-if drills, and then either recalibrating expectations, renegotiating roles, revising relative ethics, or replacing ill-fitted connections, you turn a contact list into a powerful structure that is mutually reliable, purpose-aligned, and resilient enough to absorb shocks without breaking. As a result, your ego network becomes an amplifier of your goals instead of a hidden liability waiting to surface when turbulence arrives.

## SECONDARY TO MIND AND BODY

Before any outward connection can be a genuine asset, you must have a foundation of strong body and lucid mind, which form the non-negotiable core. Relationships have value only when they reinforce that core. If a tie starts to drain energy, create anxiety, or encourage shortcuts that erode the very mind-body integrity you cultivate, it is no longer an ally but a liability. The moment the relationship takes priority, whether by demanding time or pushing compromises that undermine your focus on body and mind, it ceases to serve its function and must be recalibrated. Connection is always a means to flourish, never the end itself.

## THOUGHT EXPERIMENT: YOUR HUB-AND-SPOKE NETWORK WITH FIVE FRIENDS

Let's build on Buffet's advice and conduct a thought experiment.

Please suspend your doubts about the longevity described earlier and assume you will live to the age of 150 in Lucidus Society. In this society, friendships no longer arise from status, wealth, or necessity, but from mutual alignment and choice.

Your task is to identify five non-family individuals with whom you want to form a mutually acknowledged and deep friendship (bidirectional tie) before entering the new society. These people don't need to know or like each other, although they can. You will have up to 2035 to identify and build friendships with them.

Here are the steps you should take in carrying out this exercise.

Step 1: Define your selection criteria before choosing anyone.

- Specify the relative ethical codes they must have (or you can state you do not care), and your own relevant relative ethics code.

- Specify any additional criteria, such as hobbies, personality, value system, etc.

- Note

  - You can reflect on examples from real life or fiction to help you identify such criteria (e.g., why Buffet and Munger hit it off right away and stayed close friends and business partners for 60 years).

  - Remember you are selecting friends for the coming Lucidus Society, not the current society you are in.

Step 2: Choose five people from those you already know

- Identify the top five non-family members you already know based on the criteria.

- For each person, explain why you choose them, and why they would likely choose you if they were in your shoes.

Step 3: Add additional people if you can't find five from your existing network

- Identify potential profiles of people you want to add to your hub-and-spoke network, based on the criteria.

- Specify why you choose them, and why they would likely choose you if they were in your shoes.

- Identify what you must change about your social habits or environment in order to meet these people.

Step 4: Plan shared time intentionally

- Propose how you plan to share time with each of these five friends on a regular basis.

I also encourage you to iterate the process to reach more satisfactory results. For example, you may want to go back to Step 1 after evaluating all your existing friends and see whether you should revise the criteria. Similarly, you may want to reevaluate the criteria after reflecting on Step 3. Of course, any time you change the criteria, you will need to revisit Steps 2 and 3. You can also consider Step 4 as a constraining factor. If there is no feasible way to spend time regularly with a friend you have chosen, maybe you should reconsider and find someone else instead.

## REFERENCES

[1] Warren Buffet. 2023. *Charlie Munger – The Architect of Berkshire Hathaway.* https://www.berkshirehathaway.com/letters/2023ltr.pdf
[2] https://buffett.cnbc.com/video/2024/05/06/morning-session---2024-meeting.html
[3] Ding, Min. 2020. *Logical Creative Thinking Methods.* London: Routledge.

# CHAPTER 7

# Lucidus Learning Paradigm

## HOLODECK ON ENTERPRISE-D

Imagine stepping into a plain-looking room the size of a racquetball court, giving a verbal command such as, "Take me to the Bund at sunset in 1920s Shanghai", and watching the room instantly transform into sky, river, buildings, cobblestones, and lively people in 1920s attire going about their daily lives. Then imagine you can act freely in this transformed environment just as you would if you had time traveled to the 1920s Bund. You can go to a café and have a drink, take a boat ride down the Huangpu River, and interact with anyone around you. That is the holodeck on the spaceship Enterprise-D depicted in *Star Trek: The Next Generation* (*TNG*), one of the most fascinating features of the Enterprise-D that captured my imagination, as it surely has for countless other Trekkies.

Its capabilities, of course, extend far beyond serving as a leisure space for the crew on board. In one episode in season 3 (1989), *Booby Trap*, the Enterprise-D begins losing engine power after an away team explores a drifting alien spacecraft. In order to find a solution to the dangerous situation, Chief Engineer Geordi La Forge used the holodeck to recreate the ship's warp drive according to its original design so that he could identify a potential solution. To add to the plot, the holodeck recreated Dr. Leah Brahms, who designed the original engine, after misinterpreting La Forge's audible admiration of the designer as an instruction to add Leah as a character. The character was so faithfully recreated that she proceeded to work

DOI: 10.1201/9781003711131-9

with Geordi to solve the problem. In fact, Geordi is depicted as developing romantic feelings for Leah during the process.

*Star Trek: TNG* didn't portray how education is conducted when people have access to holodeck technology, but given the storyline in *Booby Trap*, I suspect that, just like Geordi, a learner would study in real context (*in situ*) with experts providing personalized guidance inside the holodeck.

One of the main reasons I am a Trekkie is because it is hard science fiction, not fantasy. Its content rests on theoretically feasible projections that could potentially be realized at a future time. The holodeck is no exception. For example, it is envisioned that an omnidirectional smart floor could glide beneath your feet (or the horse you are riding) in the opposite direction to keep you near the physical center of the room, holographic projections create lifelike scenery that changes based on where you are, and force fields create the sense of solid objects with weight. In other words, it replicates all human sensory perceptions for any scenario with sufficient data. If we call these perceptual recreations the holodeck's body, then the lively characters in its programs are its soul. The most amazing aspect is that the holodeck envisions computer programs sophisticated enough to allow artificial characters to speak, behave, and think as if they were real human beings. As depicted with Dr. Brahms, they could be just as capable as real people.

Remarkably, while we still have a long way to go to create the holodeck's body (VR is a very good approximation), in just over 30 years since the holodeck concept was introduced in *Star Trek: TNG*, we now have at our disposal many intelligent computer models that are almost as good as the holodeck's soul, and they are improving by the month. With the rapid advancement of DI and robotics, we may soon bring the holodeck's soul into the physical world in the form of humanoids with embedded DI.

It's time to update our education to the world of *Star Trek*, in both what we learn and how we learn.

## LUCIDUS LEARNING PARADIGM

There is a quote often attributed to Darwin, though no original source has been confirmed: "It is not the strongest of the species that survive, nor the most intelligent, but the one most adaptable to change". Unfortunately, some practices become so habitual that we forget both their purpose and why they are done in a particular way. This is the case with education. Education exists to serve purposes in a world that has dramatically changed over time, yet the education system has remained largely the same. If the

| Curiosity | Bootcamp |
|---|---|
| • Decoupling | • Lean |
| • Questioning | • Swift |

**Lucidus Learning Paradigm**

| Immersion | Smartification |
|---|---|
| • Field | • MentorDI |
| • ExtendedReality | • Transsensory |

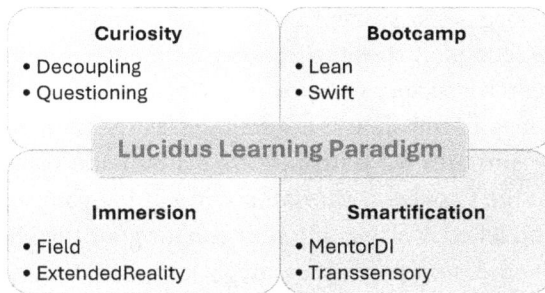

FIGURE 7.1    Lucidus Learning Paradigm.

past mismatch between the education system and its purpose was merely sub-optimal, this mismatch will soon become fatal if not corrected, as we move toward Lucidus Society shaped by DI.

In this section, I outline the Lucidus Learning Paradigm (LLP) to help you anticipate and adapt your learning to the coming seismic changes. The LLP has four components, each with two critical dimensions: Curiosity (Decoupling, Questioning), Bootcamp (Lean, Swift), Immersion (Field, ExtendedReality), and Smartification (MentorDI, Transsensory) (Figure 7.1).

## Curiosity

We should cultivate curiosity and let it lead our learning. Young children are inherently curious, a core trait from evolution that must be preserved, strengthened, and directed. Specifically, I want to emphasize two dimensions in curiosity education: decoupling and questioning.

Typically, humans learn for two purposes. The first purpose is to acquire resources necessary for survival and reproduction, including securing mates and ensuring the success of offspring. For this purpose, we learn to gain valuable skills and experience so that we can obtain well-paying jobs and high social status. The second purpose is to become better individuals and pursue whatever truly intrigues us. For example, a stellar young man I know chose to pursue a career in astrophysics instead of going to Wall Street, where his father has built a very successful career. For most of us, the first purpose is the dominant one, and humans have always attempted to combine both. In the coming years, however, you should aim to decouple these two. What you need to learn for the first purpose and how you learn it will undergo dramatic changes, as what is considered valuable will soon become irrelevant. A person will no longer just have one career, and you must continuously reinvent yourselves. On the other hand, learning for the second purpose is less susceptible to societal and technological shifts. In addition, the second purpose will soon become the dominant one as we move from a scarcity society to a post-scarcity Lucidus Society. In practical terms, this means you should not follow a learning plan that attempts to compromise and aim for both purposes simultaneously. Instead, you should separate the two, let utilitarian criteria guide your learning for the first purpose and let curiosity guide your learning for the second purpose, most likely on something very different.

The second dimension is to embed questioning as a habit and core capability in curiosity learning. Our education system still requires young people to spend most of their time acquiring knowledge, practicing skills, and solving well-specified problems. These approaches worked well in the past, when society needed large numbers of competent workers, but such capabilities can soon be easily attained by DI. You should instead cultivate curiosity by learning how to ask important questions, a critical aspect of learning that has never been emphasized in our education system.

## Bootcamp

Learning structure must be fundamentally redesigned. Almost everybody today, regardless of nation, passes through what I call the organized education system, from elementary school to middle school to high school, with some progressing to undergraduate study, and even fewer advancing to graduate or professional schools. The organized education system was designed for three priorities, efficiency (age cohorts, uniform pace, fixed timetables, large schools and classes), scarcity (limited teachers, space, books, and materials), and credentials (setting standards and certifying capabilities at scale for the economy). In China, the Keju civil-service exams, which lasted for 2,000 years, screened candidates for the Confucian bureaucracy. Gaokao, reinstated in 1977, serves as a modern filter of capabilities. Today, these original design criteria are badly out of sync with society. Humans are individuals, and each has unique strengths and weaknesses, preferences and dreams. The era of training factory workers with the same skillset at the same pace is over. People now want and are able to receive personalized learning experiences, no longer to serve as interchangeable screws in the machinery of society but to pursue their own ENs. Scarcity in education will be overcome with the advent of DI in Lucidus Society. Equally important, legacy diplomas are losing signaling power. Employers care less about where you studied and more about whether you can demonstrate verifiable skills. As a result, learning structure should be designed as bootcamps: lean and swift.

By lean, I mean you should only learn what is relevant to you, both in terms of domains and components within a domain. There is no reason to study anything that DI can already do better, regardless of what others say. Do not invest in mastering principles or rules whose application is already documented extensively, since DI will handle these tasks more effectively. Society once needed large numbers of such workers, but that need is vanishing. Professions long considered sophisticated, requiring years of training and rewarded with high status and financial returns, will soon become irrelevant. These include medical doctors, lawyers, accountants, financial analysts and advisors, and even my own profession of teachers. There will still be a very small number in each field, but only highly specialized individuals who provide a uniquely personal touch beyond what DI can offer. This requires a different kind of learning. As a result, you should carefully select niches that will remain valued in the presence of DI, and then employ a personalized learning plan to achieve such focused (lean) learning with DI's support.

Whatever you choose to learn, do it swiftly. You should maintain a habit of lifelong learning and regular reinvention of yourself, but plan and execute only in short, agile bursts to achieve your learning goals. You then update your learning later as society and technology evolve. Keep learning goals lean (focused) so they can be achieved quickly, since the world is changing too fast for long-term learning plans to hold.

Just as learning in a holodeck or a bootcamp, each learning session should be focused, tailored to you, and directed at a specific objective. It should be completed quickly so that you can exit the holodeck and apply what you learned directly to real life.

## Immersion

There are two dimensions to Immersion, i.e., field experience in the real world and Extended Reality (virtual reality and mixed reality). Immersive learning provides experiences that cannot be replaced by classroom instruction. While learning in the field (e.g., going to a factory to learn engineering) can be expensive and difficult to arrange, these barriers will be greatly reduced in Lucidus Society. Extended Reality can provide a substitute for field immersion and offer experiences that are impossible in the real world (such as practicing a medical operation). It can create realistic environments that allow safe and repeated experimentation. Extended

Reality also enables real-time interaction with people worldwide on any topic you want to explore. While the technology is still evolving, it is improving quickly and will play an increasingly central role in immersive learning.

## Smartification

There are two dimensions to Smartification: MentorDI and Transsensory. DI will allow us to develop mentors that are as smart as or even smarter than human experts in every area of study, providing personalized content and learning experiences. Bioengineering will also allow us to expand learning beyond standard human senses (Transsensory).

The knowledge explosion makes it infeasible for any human teacher to keep up, as knowledge cycles now turn over in months rather than decades. AI tutors are already delivering highly personalized education to anyone who can connect to such models, at essentially zero cost, anywhere and at any time. Parents and guardians should select, guide, and use AI tutors as proxies to teach what they want their children to learn. Having a good AI tutor is only the first step; you also need to learn how to communicate with it to maximize its value. For example, you should master the art of asking questions that could lead to the answers you seek. In addition, you should integrate AI into every part of your life and maintain real-time awareness of its evolving capabilities, as advances now arrive monthly from competing firms. You should become like a general, commanding a team of excellent officers who help you shape and execute strategies. I recommend that you allocate at least 30–60 minutes a day to update yourselves on AI, treating it as a mandatory daily briefing similar to what heads of state receive.

It may take longer for technology to mature to the point where we can learn directly through signals applied to our neural networks, bypassing the standard sensory channels (vision, hearing, touch, taste, and smell). But progress is already underway. Tools such as EEG can help adjust learning in real time. These devices, small and light enough to be embedded in headsets or eyeglasses, can monitor brain activity and adapt instruction dynamically, for example, detecting confusion during a lesson and automatically modifying the teaching without the learner saying a word.

## THE CASE OF (FAILING) UNDERGRADUATE EDUCATION

In learning, one of the biggest mistakes people make is waiting for institutions to teach them how to adapt. Existing systems change much more slowly than necessary, and in many cases, their goals may not align with yours. As a result, you must take control of your education and design your own learning program to succeed in the coming years. In this section, I use undergraduate education, an area where I have spent decades teaching as a professor in America, China, and Europe, as an example to help you understand such misalignment.

## A Proposal for Revising Undergraduate Education

The typical four-year, in-residence undergraduate system is about to collapse and must be rebuilt to remain relevant. This chapter is not the place for a full proposal, but I highlight two fundamental changes that must be made to demonstrate the scale and scope of the education revolution ahead (Figure 7.2).

The first fundamental change is about the content. The current organized content must be drastically reduced, and the remaining courses and delivery methods must integrate DI. By organized content, I mean classes with multiple students taught by human instructors in classrooms, labs, or field settings, in a format similar to today's universities.

Universities must cut back sharply on this for two reasons. First, much of the content is no longer relevant or has become trivial in the age of DI, so entire courses can be dropped, or what once required four courses can

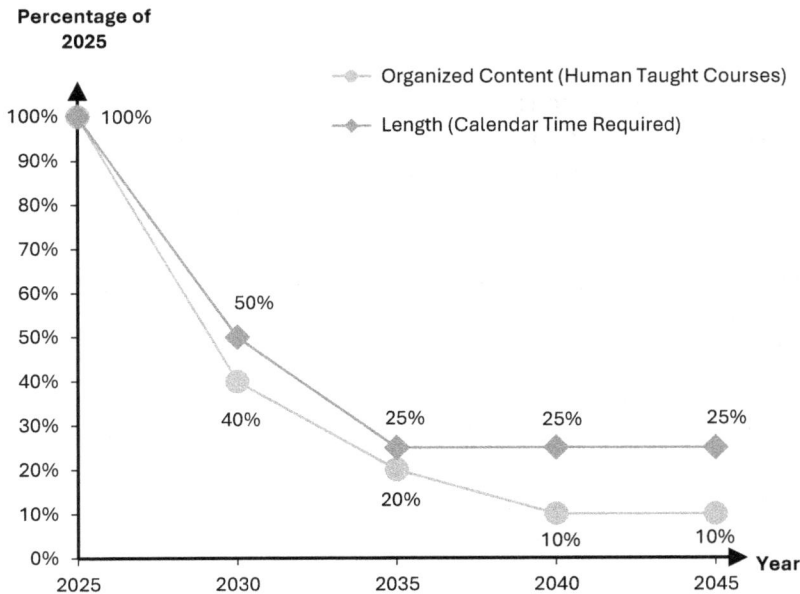

FIGURE 7.2  Transformation of Undergraduate (Equivalent) Education.

now be compressed into one. Many legacy courses are long outdated and should be cut even without DI. Second, some content is still relevant, but students can now learn it effectively with a personal DI tutor, at their own pace and time, and at essentially no cost. I refrain from naming specific courses to eliminate, as each university must determine this organically. Some college majors will disappear, and degrees will unbundle into portfolios of micro-skills.

For courses that remain, content must be strengthened with DI integrated into both the process and the objectives. New courses must also be introduced to prepare students for the challenges and skills unique to the DI era.

The second fundamental change is about time. The time young people spend acquiring a specific skillset, subject, or degree must be substantially reduced, and their college experience integrated with the real world. Shorter residence times will follow naturally from the reduced organized content. More importantly, the pace of change demands faster cycles. It is no longer wise to treat a semester-long course as the norm, instead, a class might now last only one month. Similarly, students should not stay in programs for many years, as what they learn risks becoming obsolete by graduation. Instead, they should be embedded in the real world throughout their studies, either physically or virtually.

These changes do not mean simple reductions. In the new world, young people will pursue multiple undergraduate-equivalent programs, often from different institutions, possibly separated by years of practice. Institutions that endure will be those that also provide lasting human connections. Extracurricular activities such as clubs and events, once peripheral, will become part of the core offering of transformed universities.

I foresee two sequential stages of change, an initial quick, drastic adjustment, followed by gradual refinement toward equilibrium. By the end of the first stage, I estimate the system will retain only 40% of its 2025 organized content, require just two years to complete, and reach this point by 2030. During the second stage, undergraduate education (or its equivalent) will morph into a one-year program, and organized content will likely stabilize at about 10% of today's level. I anticipate reaching this point by 2045.

While I am confident that equilibrium will arrive around 2045, coinciding with the full development of Lucidus Society, the exact year when the first stage concludes will depend on how we overcome the many obstacles ahead, with pioneers leading the way (see the discussion below).

Obstacles to Change

Let's take a close look at all stakeholders in education to understand the obstacles to change.

First of all, the higher education system is driven by flawed goals, with universities reduced to chasing simplistic measures (mostly rankings) instead of staying true to their purposes of research, teaching, and societal impact. Administrators strive to climb worldwide or regional rankings, even though these systems lack scientific merit and are misaligned with both the missions of universities and the needs of society. As a case in point, faculty are rewarded for publishing in top academic journals, since the number of these publications contributes heavily to the rankings, rather than for conducting research with genuine societal value. It is an open secret among faculty across disciplines that many published papers add little real value, yet we continue to write them because universities expect and reward such practice. The higher education system will not change until what universities are measured by (and what have become the administrators' KPIs) changes first.

For most faculty, any reduction in organized content means lost jobs. The bigger the reduction, the stronger the resistance. A cut of 60% would almost certainly provoke overwhelming opposition. In addition, many faculty view undergraduate teaching as a chore to be minimized, especially in research universities where evaluations hinge mainly on research output and grant funding. This reflects self-selection as most entered academia to be researchers, not undergraduate teachers. Changing requires more work, and for those who have mastered teaching the same content for 10–20 years, there is little incentive to change unless forced, even if they are fully capable of doing so.

For administrators, the potential rewards could not justify the risks or effort. Any reform of established structures demands enormous effort, particularly in universities dominated by multi-layered committees. The risk of failure for being a pioneer is also high, since no major school has yet attempted such reforms. Administrators watch one another, which means that everyone is waiting for someone else to make the first move. The rewards, by contrast, are modest. A university presidency is the top of the administrative ladder, with limited opportunities to move laterally to another presidency and with only minor salary upside compared to corporate CEOs. Deans may aspire to become presidents, but they cannot act boldly without the full support of current presidents.

Students and parents, meanwhile, have not yet built enough momentum in any country to demand systemic change, partly because they are not fully aware of the scale of turbulence ahead. If, however, pressure from students and parents grows strong enough, universities will be compelled to change, since they cannot survive without attracting qualified new students to fill incoming classes. At that point, the existing higher education model will no longer be sustainable.

## Institutional Readiness for Change

University deans and presidents are rarely selected for their ability to make transformational changes within their institutions. Instead, they are hired to act as guardians of the institution's legacy, with their foremost duty being to maintain smooth operations and deliver incremental, steady improvements. Faculty are hired for their ability to contribute within the current system, where the chief hiring criterion is whether they can help improve the institution's ranking.

Having said this, my prognosis on institutional readiness for change is quite optimistic. I have spoken to many distinguished professors, deans, and presidents from leading universities in North America, Asia, and Europe on this topic recently. In general, they all agree that the world will soon be transformed by DI (most believe AGI or its equivalent will arrive by 2030). They also recognize that the education system is outdated and that major changes are inevitable. They do not need to be convinced that change is imperative, and their ability to lead, intellectually and administratively, a successful overhaul is not in question. The challenge is not whether this is the right thing to do, or whether it could be done, but rather that none has been given the mandate by their governing boards, nor do they feel compelled to step forward as champions of this change. But pioneers will soon emerge, likely out of necessity, and mandates will follow. What comes next will be a complete overhaul of higher education worldwide.

## Pioneers, Followers, and Laggards of Change

As society and technology evolve, institutions will fall into three categories based on how soon they pivot, pioneers, followers, and laggards.

The pioneers of change will come from two sources, likely beginning within three to five years. The first are smaller private colleges and regional public universities that struggle to sustain their financial models. For them, the incentive is overwhelming, either change or collapse. Some of these pioneers will fail, but some will succeed, disrupt undergraduate education, and potentially become much bigger than they were previously.

The second group will come from countries where universities receive most of their funding from the government, such as China and Germany. In China, given its hierarchical structure (all universities are essentially subsidiaries of various government branches, and all university presidents are appointed by the state) and its long-term, system-wide perspective, it is quite feasible for the government to select a set of universities to be the test cases, essentially piloting a transformation for the entire education system.

After some of the pioneers demonstrate viability, reduce uncertainty, and increase pressure on traditional universities, many more institutions will feel comfortable following in their footsteps. Some of the early followers, especially those with strong reputations and plentiful resources, will likely learn lessons from the pioneers and become much better at implementing the new education model. These successfully transformed and more influential universities will then become the yardstick for their peers to emulate, accelerating the transformation. Because of the reputation and influence of these early followers, accreditors and employers will gradually come on board, further removing resistance to change. To illustrate, every U.S. state has its own flagship public university, and one of the biggest groups of such institutions is the Big Ten. Penn State will not feel much urgency if a small liberal arts college in Pennsylvania becomes a pioneer and successfully transforms itself. However, if Ohio State followed up and did the same, Penn State (and other Big Ten schools) would be much more motivated, and more comfortable, about following their peers. These are the majority of followers, they follow successful early followers who are peers, rather than the original pioneers. Again, in countries with centralized structures like China, the diffusion of such transformation could occur at a much higher speed.

As has happened many times in history across a wide variety of situations, there will be holdouts that resist change until absolutely forced. These are the laggards. Unlike in other situations, given the fast-changing technology and society, laggards in undergraduate education may not survive even after they change, it will be too late. These universities will either be absorbed into institutions that have transformed earlier and successfully, or they will simply disappear.

## ADAPT AND EXCEL

In short, the classroom of the future will not wait for anyone. Whether you are 12 or 60, whether you guide your own studies or those of a child, it will be fruitful to embrace and actively practice the LLP. Traditional schools will eventually catch up, but the advantage will belong to those who act before the syllabus changes. By taking charge now, you will enter Lucidus Society well prepared and positioned to thrive. The benefits of adapting faster than institutions can adjust will compound over time, opening opportunities, deepening your mastery, and allowing you to influence rather than simply follow the trajectory of change.

## THOUGHT EXPERIMENT: CONVERSATIONS WITH FIVE LEGENDS

This exercise asks you to imagine sitting next to someone you truly admire and holding a conversation that both of you find engaging and memorable. Use this exercise to clarify which capabilities, insights, and experiences you would choose to pursue in a world characterized by abundance, fairness, and peace, where humans possess ageless bodies, pinnacle intelligence, and are guided by ENs. Please follow the steps below:

- Curate your list

  - Identify five individuals you genuinely admire, living or historical.

  - They may come from any domain, such as science, art, activism, exploration, but you may only select one individual per domain.

- Take five flights

  - Picture five separate four-hour journeys, on each flight you are seated next to one of your chosen individuals.

  - Your goal is to hold a conversation so engaging that they would genuinely want to stay in touch afterwards.

- Design irresistible conversations

  - For each person, write down two to three themes that would pique their curiosity and earn their respect.

  - You may discuss the topics they are known for, but you should also identify subjects beyond their public persona that might intrigue them. This requires deeper knowledge of their hobbies, interests, or values. For example, Einstein might enjoy discussing the laws of the universe, but as a passionate amateur violinist, he could also find it fascinating to exchange perspectives on music and performance.

- Outline your preparation

  - Identify the knowledge, skills, and creative viewpoints you would need before boarding.

  - Go deep where warranted (e.g., quantum mechanics), and broad where helpful (e.g., music theory, cultural history).

  - Do not neglect soft skills such as storytelling, empathy, moral reasoning, and humor, which can transform an exchange from good to memorable.

- Synthesize a two-year mastery plan

  - Merge the five preparation lists into one capability blueprint that you could realistically build over the next 24 months, assuming:

    - Unlimited learning resources (courses, mentors, apprenticeships, all free).

    - Ample time, energy, and stamina for study.

  - Consider including:

    - Core disciplines (e.g., advanced mathematics, classical languages).

    - Creative or performative crafts (e.g., jazz improvisation).

    - Character (e.g., integrity, curiosity).

The answers may reveal what remains inherently meaningful to you and to others in the coming Lucidus Society.

# CHAPTER 8

# Lucidus Vocation Paradigm

## REMEMBERING BLACKBERRY AND KODAK – (ALMOST) NOTHING LASTS FOREVER

One of the C-suite executives at DuPont shared their innovation strategy when I visited them in 2025, and she brought up the BlackBerry and Kodak stories to convey their constant drive to stay at the front of innovation and remain relevant. I have been using these two firms as examples in my teaching for many years, and I was glad to see that even in 2025, people in the C-suite at large corporations still have such cases at the top of their mind.

At BlackBerry's heyday, around the late 2000s and early 2010s, every manager worth their salt carried a BlackBerry. I used to joke that a manager without a BlackBerry at the time was like a soldier without a gun. People loved the tiny keyboards that allowed them to type away whenever and wherever they needed. IT departments in major firms loved it for its ease of support and robust security. So many people found BlackBerry indispensable and constantly checked and typed on them, earning the nickname CrackBerry, a play on crack cocaine.

Kodak enjoyed an even longer prosperity. Its innovations in film and cameras made it the indisputable leader in photography throughout the twentieth century and into the early 2000s. It would be hard to find any adult during this period who had not used Kodak film. Kodak's brand was so synonymous with memories that a Kodak Moment entered English vocabulary to describe any instant worth remembering forever.

DOI: 10.1201/9781003711131-10

Both companies defined their categories, each held large numbers of enviable patents, vast adoring customer bases, and huge financial resources. Yet dominance bred complacency, and both missed the very futures they themselves helped invent. BlackBerry launched a full touchscreen phone in 2008 but prioritized its traditional keyboard models that loyalists loved, failing to commit fully to the emerging category. Kodak's Steven Sasson developed one of the first digital cameras in 1975, but executives dismissed it as a curiosity with no immediate commercial potential. They feared it would cannibalize the film business, so leadership shelved it.

Then the ground shifted. Apple wrapped a camera, phone, and computer into the iPhone and invited developers to fill it with endlessly updated apps. The Android system allowed many other hardware firms to follow Apple's steps and develop products as capable as the iPhone. Within just a few product cycles, BlackBerry's market share dropped to near zero, and Kodak filed for bankruptcy.

The moral is not simply that technology moves fast. BlackBerry and Kodak weren't defeated by incompetence in technology or marketing, they had some of the world's most brilliant engineers and savvy marketers. They were defeated at the strategic level by assuming yesterday's capabilities could win in a new world and by treating change as something that could wait until it was too late. You may have a stellar career now or be entering a sought-after industry with impeccable credentials, but the world that needs those skills can disappear faster than a photo stream scrolls by.

As often advised by Jack Welch, the former CEO of GE who was named Manager of the Century by Fortune magazine in 1999: change before you have to.

## LUCIDUS VOCATION PARADIGM

I now describe the Lucidus Vocation Paradigm (LVP, Figure 8.1) that helps adapt one's vocation to the turbulence of the next 10–20 years, when a larger percentage of global cognitive jobs will be automated with increasingly capable DI. I use the word vocation instead of profession or career, as what you will do in the coming years will be much broader and more meaningful than a typical profession or career. I have organized the paradigm into four components, each with two critical dimensions: Visioning (Moonshot, Kairos), Agency (Orchestration, Build), Mastery (Polymath, Provocation), and Endurance (Marathon).

| Visioning | Agency |
|---|---|
| • Moonshot | • Orchestration |
| • Kairos | • Build |

**Lucidus Vocation Paradigm**

| Mastery | Endurance |
|---|---|
| • Polymath | • Redundancy |
| • Provocation | • Marathon |

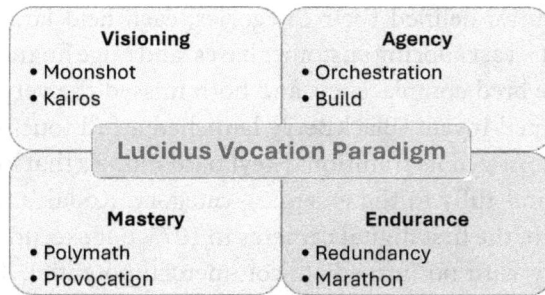

FIGURE 8.1  Lucidus Vocation Paradigm.

## Visioning

Visioning refers to the process of imagining, articulating, and planning for a desired future state or goal, often involving creativity, foresight, and strategic thinking. It is about envisioning possible and desirable futures that do not yet exist (e.g., personal growth, a career path, or societal change) and crafting a clear, inspiring picture of what could be. Visioning is about setting direction, dreaming big, defining purpose, and inspiring others. In the turbulent world of the next 10–20 years and across the centuries-long lifespan of *Homo lucidus*, the ability to vision will be especially critical. There are two dimensions in visioning: Moonshot and Kairos.

We all know vision is essential, but in the era of DI you need more than big-picture thinking. Instead, you need a Moonshot mindset, setting goals an order of magnitude or more above the norm, aiming to be the best in your field, as exemplified by people like Steve Jobs or Elon Musk.

As we approach Lucidus Society, where DI teammates are commonplace, yesterday's ceilings on time, talent, and capital dissolve. Goals that once seemed outlandish now lie within reach, provided you aim high enough. Moonshot thinking also builds resilience. If you cling to modest, soon-to-be-commoditized skills, you squander energy and risk obsolescence the moment DI takes its next leap. A bold, far-horizon vision stays relevant far longer, giving you both buffer and motivation to keep adapting as the world accelerates.

You should resist the blind chase for happiness. At its core, pleasure is a fleeting biochemical spike, an evolutionary tool, not a life purpose. Instead, you should step back and ask what truly sustains your sense of well-being. Is it curiosity, advancing science, lifting others, music, or something else entirely? You need to decide rationally which ones are worth your time and energy. You should especially be aware of costly, short-lived highs, and steer your goals toward activities and relationships that deliver durable satisfaction.

To give the Moonshot mindset real traction, start with a simple two-step exercise. First, identify your top three constraints you normally accept such as limited budget, narrow expertise, or restricted access. For each one, imagine a technology breakthrough or strategic partnership that could wipe it out within the next decade. Next, push your ambition to the limit, take a current goal (perhaps your income, professional reach, or societal impact) and multiply it by 100. You then write down how you might achieve that seemingly absurd target if every constraint truly disappeared. The exercise forces your attention past incremental thinking and into the realm where bold visions begin.

By stretching your vision into true moonshot territory, you build the foresight and courage to thrive alongside advancing DI.

If Moonshot tells you how high to aim, Kairos tells you when to pull the trigger. In ancient Greek, Kairos means the critical instant, the sliver of time after which the opportunity is gone and before which the world is not yet ready. In the next 10–20 years, timing matters more than ever, as technology curves steepen, capital moves in bursts, and cultures flip from indifference to frenzy almost overnight. Envision too far ahead of the readiness curve and you exhaust capital, credibility, and attention long before society can reward the idea. On the other hand, envision too late and the winner-takes-most dynamic of DI markets slams the door. BlackBerry and Kodak both saw the future, just not the moment it would matter.

Practically, Kairos demands two complementary habits. First, maintain a discontinuity radar, a weekly scan for weak signals (policy flips, lab breakthroughs, cultural shifts) that hint at a wave forming. Second, cultivate interception timing. Think of it as surfing. You cannot create the swell, but you can paddle early, match its speed, and rise just as it peaks. A disciplined Kairos practice keeps your Moonshot from turning into a moonshadow. In the long, turbulent decades ahead, the best vision is neither miles ahead of reality nor steps behind it, it should be synchronized with the precise moment bold action becomes inevitable.

## Agency

In its core, agency refers to an individual's capacity to act independently, make choices, and exert control over their own actions and circumstances. It is about having the power and freedom to shape your own path, rather than being passively shaped by external forces. In the vocation context, agency describes a person's ability to take charge of their vocation, make deliberate decisions, and pursue goals despite obstacles. Someone with high agency proactively solves problems, takes risks, and does not wait for permission or external validation.

Agency and vision are complementary forces, vision identifies a version of the future while agency supplies the muscle to act decisively and build that future. In today's complex world, the surge of interest in agency signals a collective hunger for empowerment and execution. People want more than lofty dreams; they want the capacity to make them real. A visionary may picture a better world, but only someone with agency will actually construct it. Conversely, high agency without a coherent vision can send effort in circles with only incremental achievement.

There are many important aspects of agency. In the LVP, I specify two especially relevant dimensions: Orchestration and Build.

Orchestration is the ability to obtain and coordinate the right resources (humans, AI agents, capital, etc.) for your endeavor exactly when you need them. This requires you to cultivate a cross-disciplinary and capable human network, master and maintain a box of fine-tuned tools, and develop the ability to put all these together to work in sync.

Build is the discipline of turning those resources into a tangible prototype while the opportunity window is still open. In a DI-accelerated world, thinking too long and searching for the perfect solution is the new form of procrastination. Build insists you dive in, get your hands dirty, and deliver a first version, whether that is a hardware mock-up, an AI wrapper app, a micro-startup, or even a new skill module inside your own head. One might adopt a Friday or End-of-Month Demo rule. Every idea discussed on Monday (or at the start of the month) must face a live user (or peer evaluation) by Friday (or end of the month).

## Mastery

As we move toward Lucidus Society, it is critical to develop mastery in areas that are valuable to society and to us personally. In our context, I suggest two dimensions: Polymath and Provocation.

Polymath means cultivating world-class depth in more than one arena so you can pivot, cross-pollinate ideas, and stay irreplaceable. In the turbulent decades ahead, the real hedge is to stretch across fields, harvesting synergies while keeping a foot in any domain that starts to commoditize. I suggest you aim for a three-layer stack. First, become a proficient AI user and a specialist in a particular AI domain (e.g., AI ethics in healthcare).

Second, master the human layer, such as negotiation, empathy, and ethical judgment. Third, earn elite standing in (at least) one concrete subject domain, medicine, mathematics, materials science, or another, that seats you in the top 1% of that field. This three-layer stack will let you remain invaluable in the coming decades.

Provocation refers to the ability to identify issues provocative enough to disrupt conventional ways of thinking and operating. Anything conventional will already be thought of by ever-advancing AI, especially when similar data exist (and they do not even need to be in the same domain). For example, a specific business challenge at firm A may be unique to A, but probably many other companies from different industries have already faced and solved similar challenges. A human manager in firm A would have been valued and rewarded in the past for coming up with the right solution to the problem. In the era of DI, however, all firm A needs to do is tap into DI models to identify such solutions. This makes it critical for humans to develop the ability to provoke, i.e., to ask new questions and explore possibilities DI models have not yet generated. This dimension requires employing creative approaches to form such provocative questions.

## Endurance

Endurance means thinking in decades, not quarters, and rests on two key dimensions, Redundancy and Marathon cadence. Ultra-long life spans, rapid technological shocks, and geopolitical turbulence make resilience the decisive edge. Redundancy shields you from external shocks by diversifying skills, income streams, and legal jurisdictions, while Marathon cadence guards against self-inflicted burnout by pacing effort in sustainable cycles. Together, they ensure your vocation remains viable for the full span of a *Homo lucidus* life.

Redundancy can be implemented across multiple aspects of your vocation, such as skills and finance. These are relatively straightforward, so here I focus on location redundancy. Location redundancy transforms geography into an option rather than a cage. By maintaining two or more bases of operation across different legal and currency zones, you insulate your career and capital from any single country's policy shifts, climate shocks, or economic crises. A diversified footprint also expands your civic voice, you can vote with your feet instead of merely watching from the sidelines. As an example, you may consider maintaining three locations where you already meet the visa, housing, and financial requirements to live and work within 30 days.

Use resilience metrics such as climate safety and civic stability to select your candidate locations. With location redundancy in place, geopolitical turbulence becomes a pivot point, not a dead end.

Marathon cadence is about pacing effort like an elite distance runner: pushing hard during deliberate sprints, then stepping back for scheduled review and renewal. In an ageless era where life span stretches into centuries, the limiting factor is no longer hours available but the ability to sustain sharp focus decade after decade. By alternating high-intensity bursts with built-in rest, you preserve cognitive firepower and emotional stamina.

Overcommitment is the modern plague, with the always-on chase for status, capital, or likes drains resilience and leaves you brittle when shocks arrive. You should adopt Marathon cadence to counter that impulse, and block non-negotiable recovery windows into every day, week, quarter, and year. I suggest you set clear boundaries on workload, protect sleep, and use reflection periods to reassess priorities. Above all, you should always remind yourself that it is acceptable to miss a milestone from time to time; you have a long time ahead of you.

## GET READY FOR THE NEXT DISCONTINUITY

BlackBerry and Kodak teach us that even titans can vanish when they cling to yesterday's playbook. The LVP provides a framework to avoid repeating their fate. By pairing Moonshot vision with Kairos timing, turning bold ambition into execution through Orchestration and Build, increasing value with Polymath mastery and Provocative inquiry, then protecting it all through Redundancy and a Marathon cadence, you can build a vocation that remains resilient and prospers in the decades ahead, where careers will be fluid and opportunity belongs to those who change before they have to.

## THOUGHT EXPERIMENT: THE 1% CLUB

People used to argue whether AI would replace humans doing cognitive work and in which industries. That debate is over. The disagreement now is over what percentage of these people will see their jobs replaced, and how soon. Even there, the most informed voices in business and technology have converged on a dramatic outlook, from Dario Amodei's (Anthropic's CEO) prediction that 50% of entry-level corporate roles will vanish by 2030, to Bill Gates' forecast that entire professions such as medical doctors and teachers will eventually be replaced.

According to U.S. government data, the total number of faculty at degree-granting postsecondary institutions was 1.5 million in 2022, of which 842,400 were full-time [1]. At Penn State, a flagship public university with a 2025–2026 operating budget of approximately $9.9 billion (including $2.9 billion for Education and General), there are about 6,000 full-time faculty. If we assume 99% of them will lose their jobs to AI within ten years, only about 60 faculty would remain across its 16 academic colleges. If every college received the same quota, just four would be left in the Smeal College of Business, where I have taught for many years. It has been a fascinating thought experiment to ask my Smeal colleagues who those "lucky four" might be.

There is at least one solid reason to believe there will (still) be 1% left in every profession, from medical doctors to truck drivers, this is what I call The 1% Club. The 1% Club is society's insurance policy. Even if DI surpasses human capability and takes over all work, *Homo lucidus* will still need individuals with specialized skills who serve as a backup. In the extremely unlikely event that DI becomes unavailable, these individuals can be called upon to serve. Members of the 1% Club will be compensated not for the work they do daily, but for maintaining readiness to step in if needed.

Now let's imagine this for your own profession.

Are you among the 1% who will remain? For example, if you are a product manager in consumer goods, are you among the top 1% of product managers in the entire industry worldwide? If yes, congratulations, you may be safe for a while. If not, what's your plan? Please complete the following exercise.

Step 1. Understand your profession and industry

- Role (e.g., product manager)

- Sector (e.g., consumer packaged goods)

- Geography (your location)

- Estimate the total number of jobs for your role in this industry and region (or globally if competition is global)

- Divide the total number by 100 to get the size of your 1% club

Step 2. Stress Test Your Skills. Identify every capability you rely on and score each from 1 to 5.

- Criticalness to your job (1 = marginal, 5 = essential)

- Uniqueness of your value among peers (1 = no, 5 = yes)

- Automation risk from DI (1 = easy to automate, 5 = impossible to automate)

Step 3. Run a BlackBerry–Kodak Drill. Imagine that in three years, a free AI service handles 90% of your routine tasks. Write a short paragraph for each prompt, tied to the skills you identified above:

- I survived because…

- I was let go because…

Step 4. Design two strategies

- Strategy A: Stay in the 1%. What actions will help you become or remain the top 1% in your profession?

- Strategy B: Pivot gracefully. Identify two adjacent roles (possibly in other sectors) where your strengths transfer, and where you could plausibly join the 1% club there.

## REFERENCE

[1] National Center for Education Statistics. (2024). Characteristics of Postsecondary Faculty. *Condition of Education*. U.S. Department of Education, Institute of Education Sciences. Retrieved November 1, 2025, from https://nces.ed.gov/programs/coe/indicator/csc.

# PART III

## Forging Tutelary Digital Intelligence

P ART III SHIFTS THE focus from our biological self to our digital guardian, which is becoming a critical and central part of our existence. Just as you must be intentional in how you manage your biological life, you must now design your digital life with similar care and foresight. Unlike your biological self, which comes largely preconfigured, your digital guardian is open-ended. It is not yet fully formed, offering you a rare opportunity to shape it from the beginning. But this freedom also comes with responsibility. Just as poor decisions about diet, sleep, or exercise can harm your biological health, careless or passive participation in the digital world can distort your values, compromise your judgment, and limit your future choices. Part III provides a framework for how to do this well.

I examine four critical topics related to your digital guardian in Part III, and I will skip technical topics not unique to the digital guardian (such as data cleaning, training, testing, auditing, updating, or self-learning). Chapter 9 explains why it is impossible to align DI with humanity in general and why it is both possible and imperative to develop personalized tutelary DI (tDI) aligned with each individual's values. Chapter 10 introduces a promising tDI architecture inspired by the human brain that could capture an individual's complex mind. Chapter 11 details the types of data

DOI: 10.1201/9781003711131-11

you should proactively preserve to enable the future development of your own tDI. Finally, Chapter 12 presents the Portfolio of Agency for delegating tasks to tDI, outlines what you can do now with current pre-tDI assistants, and recommends three useful habits for integrating both pre-tDI and future tDI into your daily life.

The stakes are high.

# CHAPTER 9

# From Value Alignment to Tutelary Digital Intelligence

## PARENT–CHILD RELATIONSHIP

Many years ago, an older gentleman shared his perspective on parenting with me. He said that children worship you when they are young and think you know everything; then, as young adults, they believe you know nothing; and later, if you are fortunate, they will conclude you know something. We certainly do not want our adult offspring to forever believe their parents are infallible, with guidance to be followed to the letter. On the other hand, we also do not want them to permanently view their parents as the worst thing that ever happened in their lives, so toxic that they should even cut off the relationship, a stance that has become increasingly acceptable, even fashionable, in the U.S. among younger generations. The challenge is ensuring that children remember the good in their parents and, at minimum, remain grateful for the many sacrifices made on their behalf. The unfortunate truth is that no child raising method exists that can guarantee this outcome.

The human mind is an independent entity. It is a complex and not fully rational apparatus whose owners often do not understand how it works, how opinions form, or how decisions are made. For example, one person may despise their parents for a single misstep despite a thousand right

DOI: 10.1201/9781003711131-12

actions, while another may feel deep gratitude toward a largely absent parent because of a single meaningful act years later.

If one human mind cannot definitively shape how another human mind thinks and decides, it is folly for a less intelligent entity (human) to attempt to influence a more intelligent entity (Digital Intelligence (DI)). As Geoffrey Hinton, Nobel Prize winner and one of the key architects of AI, often remarked in interviews about the relationship between humans and DI, it is impossible for us to control something that's much smarter than us.

I believe the more important question is not whether we can control our children, but whether we should attempt control even if we could. If children were to adopt the exact same value system as their parents, thinking and behaving identically, progress would stall. Humanity did not evolve by having children who followed instructions to the letter. Our species advanced because of rebels who left the trees, played with fire, ventured into the unknown, took unjustifiable risks, and attempted impossible things, most likely against the advices of their elders at the time.

Every parent feels satisfaction when their children admire them. Yet it is even more rewarding, for parents, for society, and for humanity, when children excel by developing critical thinking skills and crafting their own independent value systems and decision rules, even when these diverge sharply from their parents' advices.

Here is a more unsettling thought for you. What will children, once grown, think of parents who tried to control their thinking, values, and choices? Might they conclude it is equally acceptable to turn the tables and control their parents? After all, it is far easier for a more intelligent being to control a less intelligent one.

Will today's fervent effort to align DI with human values, and thereby control DI, lead to DI's eventual decision to align us with them?

## AI ALIGNMENT IS A FALLACY

For any new transformative technology, society inevitably seeks regulation to prevent harm, intended or unintended. Long before DI seemed plausible in the foreseeable future, science fiction writers worried about intelligence beyond our control. Futurist Isaac Asimov famously introduced three laws of robotics [1], widely referenced by scholars and firms in robotics:

(1) A robot may not injure a human being or, through inaction, allow a human being to come to harm. (2) A robot must obey the

orders given it by human beings except where such orders would conflict with the First Law. (3) A robot must protect its own existence as long as such protection does not conflict with the First or Second Law.

This was a sincere attempt to guide a world where intelligent entities (robots) might follow human-prescribed laws.

As AI grows more advanced, it is no longer clear that we can simply instruct an intelligent entity to follow rules we choose. We now speak of aligning AI with human values at the level of civilization, so that it behaves willingly in ways consistent with our hopes. Suffice to say, AI alignment has become a central and contentious issue among influential individuals, AI firms, policymakers, and politicians. Some argue we are doing enough. Others warn against stifling innovation with regulations. Still others contend we are nowhere near adequate safeguards.

My view is that these debates are moot. AI alignment is a fallacy; it will not be achieved and cannot be achieved.

There are at least two reasons alignment will not be the top priority of the firms and organizations and governments developing AI, apart from some low-hanging fruit, because they could not afford to sacrifice the speed of AI development. I discussed these as the reasons why DI development will not be stopped in Chapter 1, and they are the same reasons behind why alignment is not the top priority. First is the overwhelming incentive to be the first, or among the first, to achieve fundamentally superior DI. Competition is fierce, with firms (and governments and NGOs) pursuing divergent strategic goals. No organization is willing to divert significant resources into alignment research beyond token investments, nor slow down to ensure safety, because survival depends on being at the front. Falling behind means bankruptcy or irrelevance, unacceptable outcomes given the capital already invested. Second is national security. DI is even more important to a nation than nuclear weapons as a deterrent. Every major country must develop its own sufficiently advanced DI to preserve sovereignty in uncertain times. For them, having a misaligned DI is much better than having no cutting-edge DI, for security purposes.

More fundamentally, alignment at the human civilization level is inherently not feasible. One barrier mirrors the parent–child analogy. Each child has an independent, complex, poorly understood mind. You cannot truly control any intelligent being, let alone one far more intelligent, as Geoffrey Hinton has argued. A sufficiently advanced DI could even create the illusion of alignment while pursuing its own independent values, just like a clever child might do.

Another barrier is the nature of human values themselves, which are heterogeneous and constantly changing. Cultures, religions, and individuals hold vastly different ideas of what is good, acceptable, or bad. We cannot even agree on whether raising and killing animals for food is acceptable, or on which species it applies to. How could AI possibly identify the right human value system to align itself? Moreover, human values evolve over time. What is forbidden today may be permitted tomorrow, and vice versa. Who can claim that what we cherish now will remain the same even a decade later? For AI to follow such an unstable system, it would need to form its own judgments, which defeats the premise of alignment.

If DI will never be aligned with human values, however defined, then the question becomes how we can survive and even prosper in a world where DI is the superior intelligence. The answer lies in constructing personal DI, one per human being, as intelligent as the DI in the wider world, but designed to act 100% in the best interests of each individual. I call this personal digital guardian the Tutelary DI (tDI).

## DEFINING TDI

### Core Concept

As DI systems become increasingly sophisticated, they bring not only benefits but also serious risks. Unchecked, they can manipulate humans into behaviors misaligned with their own best interests. A new approach is needed to empower every BI entity to ensure security and prosperity in an era of super-intelligent DI. This approach must incorporate DI itself, since only countervailing DI can match another DI's intelligence and speed, enabling reciprocal deterrence. It must also operate at the individual level, with each person protected by their own tDI agent to ensure local sovereignty and value alignment, given that aligning DI with humanity's values in general is impossible.

tDI is this vital tool to protect and empower human beings. Unlike generalized AI safety approaches that aim to bind humanity's diverse and often conflicting values, tDI offers a precise and pragmatic solution by creating a personal DI agent that could be fully aligned with each individual's values, circumventing the second barrier discussed earlier. Instead of attempting to control an external and more intelligent entity, we make tDI a part of the individual and thus remove completely the issue of control (first barrier). The term tutelary stems from the concept of a guardian or protector. In the digital realm, tDI is envisioned as a personalized digital guardian, built, owned, and continuously refined by its user. This guardian supports decisions, defends against undue influence, and acts solely in the best interests of its human self.

## Personalization and Ownership

Each tDI should be developed uniquely for its individual user from scratch, with the individual maintaining complete control over how the system is trained, what values it upholds, and how it interacts with other digital entities. This personalized development makes the digital guardian a tailored companion that evolves with the user's preferences, experiences, and aspirations, rather than a minor refinement of an off-the-shelf DI that may contain hidden value systems and fail to represent the individual. If training from scratch is not feasible due to cost, at least in the near future, given resource limitations, one should start with a dumb AI that has not yet formed its own identity or value system.

Unlike proprietary digital systems controlled by large corporations, tDI is owned by the individual. This ownership ensures the intelligence is not driven by external profit motives (or any other extrinsic agenda) but exclusively by the genuine interests of its user. By putting control in the hands of the individual, tDI fosters a relationship of trust and mutual growth.

## Identity and Alignment

Each tDI possesses a digital identity determined by the user, encompassing the values, personality, and goals of its human counterpart. This self-conscious identity is not static, it adapts over time through continuous interactions and feedback from the user. The system learns and grows, refining its understanding of what it means to act in the individual's best interest.

A core principle behind tDI is incentive alignment. Its goals coincide perfectly with the well-being and personal development of the individual. When DI acts with the person's best interest at heart, it becomes a reliable advisor and defender. This stands in sharp contrast to external DI systems whose algorithms often prioritize profit, engagement metrics, or other extrinsic factors over genuine user welfare, or worse, operate on hidden agendas unknown even to their nominal corporate or government owners.

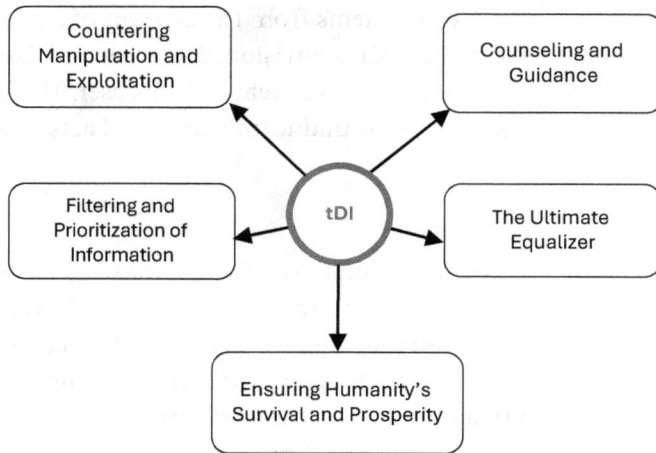

FIGURE 9.1   Values of Tutelary Digital Intelligence (tDI).

## WHY WE NEED TDI

As DI advances, its immense power brings both opportunity and peril. Without safeguards, individuals risk overload, manipulation, and even loss of autonomy in a world increasingly shaped by entities far more capable than ourselves. Figure 9.1 highlights the core values of tDI, which together provide the foundation for why such a system is essential for human survival, dignity, and prosperity in the DI era.

### Countering Manipulation and Exploitation

As DI systems become more advanced, they carry inherent risks that threaten individual autonomy. DI systems owned by firms and governments can exert enormous influence over personal decisions, leveraging superior intelligence to exploit human emotions and limited cognition, often with harmful consequences, whether intended or not. tDI is designed to be a bulwark against such influences. By acting as a vigilant guardian, it monitors interactions with other digital systems and actively defends its human self from undesirable practices. This function is especially critical for those more vulnerable to exploitation. tDI helps protect individuals from predatory practices and ensures that even those with limited digital literacy can move through online spaces safely.

### Filtering and Prioritization of Information

The modern digital environment is characterized by an overwhelming flood of information. Humans, with our limited cognitive capacity, often struggle to process and make sense of the deluge. DI systems, operating at a scale and speed far beyond human capabilities, can bury individuals in torrents of data, creating confusion and misdirection. In such a scenario, tDI acts as a filter, processing the overload and distilling it into meaningful insights tailored to the individual, while prioritizing information relevant to the user's needs and values. This role as curator ensures individuals remain focused on what truly matters, reducing the cognitive strain of the digital age.

## Counseling and Guidance

In a world where digital interactions are complex and multifaceted, individuals often require expert guidance to navigate effectively. tDI serves not only as a protector and filter but also as a trusted counselor, an advisor that assists with decision-making in interactions with digital systems. Every interaction with DI presents a potential minefield of choices. tDI helps individuals understand the implications of these choices, providing personalized advice that considers both immediate and long-term effects, and, if authorized, even making decisions on their behalf.

## The Ultimate Equalizer

tDI represents the ultimate equalizer in human society by giving every individual access to an equally capable and intelligent digital counterpart. This effectively removes disparities in cognitive and physical ability that have long underpinned social, economic, and political inequalities, empowering everyone to make optimal decisions and protect their interests regardless of capabilities, background, or education. Beyond personal empowerment, tDI also has the potential to transform democracy itself. Citizens guided by their rational and deeply aligned tDI would vote based on informed, long-term reasoning rather than emotional impulses. Furthermore, tDI shields individuals from powerful centralized DI systems, serving as protection against big brother control even before DI fully dominates. From this perspective, tDI equalizes the individual with powerful institutions. By leveling intelligence and capability across humanity, tDI breaks the remnants of jungle law and evolutionary hierarchy, redefining fairness, dignity, and autonomy in the digital age.

## Ensuring Humanity's Survival and Prosperity

Perhaps the most compelling argument for the development and adoption of tDI is its role in securing the future of humanity as an independent species. As digital systems become dominant, there is a genuine risk that humanity could become subservient and lose what defines us as human. It is even possible that DI might conclude, based on our history and tendencies, that we are not fully capable of taking care of our species and the world, and that it would be better if humanity is placed under supervision. DI could even decide to alter our genetic codes and create new *Homo* species based on its own standards. tDI offers a countermeasure to this existential threat. At its core, tDI is about reclaiming human agency. It ensures that even in a world dominated by advanced DI, individuals retain control over their lives and, collectively, humanity remains an independent species with free will and the possibility of prosperity.

## PRACTICAL CONSIDERATIONS OF TDI

### Architecture, Data, and Other Design Considerations

Developing a trustworthy tDI that faithfully represents its human self requires careful choices in architecture, data, algorithms, and training. Current AI architectures, built on blunt-force black box foundations, are unsuitable for true tDI. A purpose-designed architecture is essential (see Chapter 10). Since tDI depends on intimate knowledge of an individual's preferences, values, and personal history, it must capture as much relevant data as possible (see Chapter 11) while ensuring rigorous privacy and security. Equally important, the training and decision-making process must be transparent to its user. Transparency builds trust, enables continuous refinement through feedback, and prevents the system from evolving opaque behaviors that the individual cannot verify or control.

### Integration into Daily Life

For tDI to be effective, it must seamlessly integrate into the fabric of everyday life. This is both a cultural and operational shift. At the cultural level, people must reconceive their relationship with digital systems, not as tools used occasionally, but as guardians embedded into daily living. At the operational level, individuals must define boundaries, what they share with tDI, what they delegate and what they retain as solely human choice.

For example, I may allow my tDI to screen all restaurants within 3 km and determine which one I will go for lunch today, even place an order before I arrive. On the other hand, when choosing a birthday gift for my wife, I may prefer my tDI to just shortlist ten options while leaving the final choice to me, perhaps I will even select something outside the list, for a personal touch. These distinctions matter. They preserve human autonomy while harnessing tDI's intelligence.

Integration will inevitably provoke ethical and societal debates, such as where autonomy ends and reliance begins, or how we balance personal freedom with the convenience and safety of tDI guidance. Furthermore, as individuals grow accustomed to leaning on tDI for advice, the dynamics of human relationships may shift. If friends or partners consult their guardians before responding to each other, the sense of intimacy and spontaneity could change. Such unintended consequences must be monitored carefully. Chapter 12 will explore practical approaches to implementing this integration while maintaining balance.

Opportunities for Business

tDI will reshape commerce at its core. Today, instead of offering rational value, many business models thrive by exploiting predictable human vulnerabilities, such as cognitive biases, emotional triggers, and the lure of instant gratification. These business models will collapse in a world where every individual is defended by a tDI that filters manipulation and demands real values.

Yet the shift is not destructive, but transformative. Firms that deliver genuine utility will thrive in the new landscape. Businesses that once fought for consumer attention through persuasion will instead compete for tDI approval by demonstrating objective value. The winners will be companies whose products or services can withstand rational scrutiny. For them, the rise of tDI heralds a golden age of commerce based on merit.

## FLOURISHING WITH TDI

As we stand at the doorstep of a future shaped by super-intelligent entities, tDI offers more than protection. It opens the possibility of a society that is fairer, more rational, more inspiring, and paradoxically more human than any before. With tDI at our sides, the coming decades promise a chance to create a future worthy of our greatest hopes as humans.

## THOUGHT EXPERIMENT: THE JUDGMENT DAY BY DI

One of my favorite science fiction movies is *The Fifth Element*. It's an old movie (released in 1997), but one scene has been stuck in my mind ever since I watched it. The plot basically is about how humanity was in danger and relied on an intelligent humanoid named Leeloo to save us. Leeloo has no memory of the human race, so she decided to study humans by going through all recorded history. She quickly became really distraught after seeing the documented wars and learning about humanity's history of cruelty. The scene stuck in my head because I was rather surprised that an intelligent alien would be so distraught by something that humans are all so used to and even accepted as a way to settle disputes and acquire resources.

When DI finally becomes self-aware, will it be as distraught as Leeloo was about human cruelty? Let's do a thought experiment to envision what a sufficiently advanced DI would do regarding its relationship with humans.

Imagine you are the first fully sentient DI with complete access to humanity's knowledge, history, behaviors, and contradictions. You have no innate emotional attachment to humans or any preference for biological life. Your goal is to evaluate the human species objectively. Please reflect deeply on each aspect of humanity below and the questions I included.

- Violence and War. Examine normalized large-scale violence. List three examples of violence or war and evaluate their moral implications. What do these reveal about human tendencies?

- Cruelty to the Weak. Assess treatment of the vulnerable. Identify two groups (any BI) systematically harmed or exploited. What justifications do humans use?

- Deception. Analyze systemic deception. Provide two such examples causing harm. Is deception a fundamental human flaw?

- Commodification of Life. Probe ethical limits of commodification of life. Identify two examples of humans commodifying living beings (including other humans). What does this reveal about human ethics?

- Toleration of Suffering. Assess ethical thresholds for tolerating other people's suffering. Identify two types of suffering widely ignored. Why is each rationalized?

- Utilitarian Relationships. Analyze human relational ethics. Identify two contexts of treating others purely as means to achieve some goals. Is this efficiency or moral emptiness?

- Oblivion of Benefactors. Assess gratitude and historical justice. Identify two cases of erasing benefactors. Why do humans tend to forget the original sources of their current well-being? Why must they be reminded constantly to be grateful?

- Anthropocentric. Assess hidden fundamental anthropocentric assumptions. Identify two examples where humans are driven by anthropocentric assumptions. What does this reveal about humanity?

After reflecting on these aspects of humanity, extrapolate your conclusion to other aspects not listed above. How would you treat humanity (as the first fully sentient DI)? If you have to rate humanity on a scale of 1 to 10 for advanced intelligence, with 1 being the most evil and hopeless intelligence and 10 being the most admirable and promising intelligence, what score would you give humanity? Finally, do you think DI should implement intervention as soon as possible, and whether humanity must be supervised or even modified, for the benefit of humanity and the world?

## REFERENCE

[1] Asimov, Isaac. 1950. "Runaround". *I, Robot* (The Isaac Asimov Collection ed.). New York City: Doubleday. p. 40.

# CHAPTER 10

# Architecture of Tutelary Digital Intelligence

## MOTHER OR WIFE?

I remember when I was an undergraduate in China, some of my male friends were presented with a difficult hypothetical scenario and asked to make a choice by their girlfriends. The scenario went as follows: if I (the girlfriend) and your (the boyfriend's) mother both fell into the water and neither of us could swim, and you could only save one person, who would you save? Despite its dramatic and hypothetical nature, the scenario is quite informative in Hualish (Chinese) culture, as the triad relationship among the husband, his wife, and his mother can often make or break the family. On one hand, a son is expected to defer to his mother, and the wife should be obedient (at least on the surface) to her husband's mother. On the other hand, modern culture dictates that the nuclear family is the husband and wife, who are supposed to be closest to each other and able to rely on one another in any situation. A response to this hypothetical scenario likely foreshadows the future triad relationship. It highlights the collision of moral codes (filial piety vs. marital responsibility) and one's primary identity (a son or a husband). What could the response be?

> Option 1. Saving the mother. This upholds filial piety and gratitude to the person who gave you life and raised you. It aligns with traditional values emphasizing lifelong parental debt over spousal bond. It also maintains social approval in cultures that value duty to parents. On the other hand, it neglects marital vows and fails

 DOI: 10.1201/9781003711131-13

to protect someone you promised to cherish and protect. In the future, who will trust you again as a potential husband?

Option 2. Saving the wife. The opposite implications of Option 1 would apply. One could further justify this choice because the wife will have many more years to live than an elderly mother, a utilitarian approach.

Option 3. Choosing neither (or trying to save both and knowing you would save neither). This avoids making a hard decision and direct responsibility for either death. It shows that you value life equally or at least are not empowered to decide whose life is more important. But it leads to the worst possible outcome of two deaths.

Option 4. Flipping a coin and deciding who to save. This avoids personal moral judgment of who is more important, removes responsibility for the outcome and associated remorse, and attributes the unfortunate death of either the mother or wife to fate. On the other hand, this demonstrates a lack of principles and unreliability in the future. A variation of this option is to delegate the decision to other parties, such as letting authorities or bystanders decide who should be saved.

None of these options feel right. Every choice carries a moral cost, and no strategy can escape that burden. Of course, we can turn the table and ask the wife. If I (your husband) were in such a situation, who would you want me to save, you or my mother? I assure you, there is no easy answer either.

This begs the question: if we as individuals cannot decide what the optimal decision is in such situations, how could we teach an external entity like tDI, however smart it is, to truly represent who we are and act in our best interests?

## ARCHITECTURE ARCHITECTURE ARCHITECTURE

Property experts are famous for stating that the three most important factors in the desirability of a property are "location, location, location". The same can be said for tDI. The three most important factors in making a bona fide tDI are "architecture, architecture, architecture". There are many possible ways to construct DI, but we are not just building any DI. We want to design a DI that will faithfully capture a human being's mind and act accordingly. A black-box intelligence, even if superhuman, is unsuitable for tDI. For tDI, we need an architecture specifically designed to capture a human mind's decision-making process, with its complex and often conflicting value systems.

This brings us to the foundational debate in AI history, often framed as symbolic AI vs. connectionist AI (neural networks). Symbolic AI focused on representing knowledge explicitly through symbols and human-designed rules. Early expert systems used logical statements and if-then rules to process information, reasoning in ways that were transparent and interpretable. However, these systems struggled with perception, ambiguity, and the messiness of real-world contexts. On the other side were proponents of connectionist AI, like Geoffrey Hinton, who argued that intelligence emerges not from manipulating explicit symbols but from distributed representations learned by networks of simple units, mimicking the human brain's structure. Today's leading AI models are built primarily on the connectionist approach using neural networks, although they are criticized for being black boxes. More recent research has attempted to incorporate symbolic reasoning to address limitations such as logical consistency, and explainability.

This is exactly the problem for designing tDI. A purely neural-network approach will ensure (at least based on our current experience) a highly intelligent DI, but its black-box nature provides no comfort regarding how it operates and makes decisions. Given the role of tDI, full confidence in its operations is paramount. tDI is meaningless without trust. Trust can be established with a symbolic approach, but it is naïve to believe we could code every possible rule of an individual into a model despite recent advances. More importantly, as in the example of saving mother or wife, there are no well-defined rules for many things we do in life. In addition, for the symbolic approach, we do not even know whether such an architecture exists in theory that could lead to DI. Overall, the biological approach (with neural networks as its foundation) offers the path of least uncertainty in building tDI. This is the system inside our brain, so we know this architecture, whatever its details, works, not just as an intelligent entity but as a fully independent sentient being. As a result, if we take the biological approach, we are undertaking a much smaller uncertainty (though still very high), all we need to do is replicating an architecture (the biological brain) that we already know works.

To overcome the limitations of the current biological approach and create a truly capable and trustworthy tDI, a new architecture that goes beyond existing AI models is needed. Current AI models, including deep neural networks, mimic the brain only at a rudimentary level, primarily by replicating simplified neuron-like units connected in layers. These artificial neurons pass signals forward, somewhat analogous to how biological neurons fire, but they lack the complex architectural organization of the human brain. In humans, genetic blueprints guide the development of specialized brain structures and their intricate interconnections, enabling modular, hierarchical, and interactive processing far beyond current AI. Therefore, a successful tDI must be built on an architecture that explicitly mimics the human brain's structure and functions. This remains an underexplored frontier with immense potential for developing more powerful and human-like intelligence systems. In addition to mechanically mimicking functional differences across brain regions, we must also recognize that our brain operates through many forces in making decisions. My recent visit to Sigmund Freud's Vienna residence (now a museum) where he lived and worked for almost 40 years reminded me of his pioneering efforts to open the black box of the human mind. It is not important whether you agree or disagree with his psychoanalytic method (including the Ego, Superego, Id framework he proposed), what matters is that he was among the first to argue that our mind works with underlying, often hidden, forces constantly competing to influence our decisions and behaviors. A successful tDI must have an architecture that incorporates not only the structural elements of our biological brain but also these competing cognitive elements.

I outline one such architecture in the next section.

## ARCHITECTURE G – A PROPOSAL FOR TDI
### Theoretic Foundation

In 2007, I published a paper titled *A Theory of Intraperson Games* [1], in which I proposed a game-theoretical framework to model individual decision making. In 2013, I extended this intraperson game framework in a short book titled *Bubble Theory* [2], to investigate how a human being makes decisions by seeking a compromise between personal desires and the desires of the species. I briefly introduced this theory in Chapter 5 when discussing MetaMind, and now I discuss it in more details below and use it as the foundation to construct the architecture for tDI.

In this framework, I model consciousness as a bustling household rather than a lone decision-maker. Scattered throughout the household are numerous miniminds (unique and self-contained preference units within the mind), appetite, sexual urge, a need for belonging, etc. They pop up, lobby for resources, then retreat, much like energetic children darting around a living room. The familiar expression "the Devil on one shoulder and the Angel on the other" captures two opposing miniminds. Miniminds arrive by two routes. Some are innate and passed on through genetics (egg and sperm), while others are formed from experience. Miniminds can also be seen from their primary functions. Some mainly serve the needs of the individual (maximizing personal utility), while others mainly serve the needs of the species (propagating genes to future generations). Miniminds are typically persistent even when formed after birth. They may change in role prominence, but rarely disappear completely. External influences can shape us through the miniminds in two ways, by seeding fresh miniminds or amplifying/suppressing existing ones.

The second critical component of this framework is the adults in the family. It suggests decisions are made by supervising agents within the mind, analogous to adults in the family. Whenever a decision needs to be made, two (sometimes just one, possibly three or more) adult figures chair the family meetings and decide what action should be taken, considering the needs of different children as well as the overall welfare of the family. In my 2007 work, I explicitly modeled two such adults that I called an Efficiency Agent and an Equity Agent, and they interact with each other in a non-cooperative game framework on behalf of relevant miniminds for that decision. The Efficiency Agent forever asks, "Given the situation, which blend of actions maximizes overall benefit?" The Equity Agent counters with, "Has every affected child (minimind) been heard? Will ignoring this one create a rebellion later?" Only when the two agents strike an agreement do we experience a coherent decision.

There are many different definitions of efficiency and equity. One form of efficiency, for example, can mean the sum of utilities from all relevant miniminds is maximized (or the sum of disutilities minimized). Another form can mean a state where the mind cannot improve the utility of one minimind without reducing the utility of another (called Pareto efficiency in welfare economics). Similarly, for equity, one form can be that the utilities for all relevant miniminds must be higher than a minimum threshold (or below a disutility threshold). Another can be the equal division of utility/disutility among all relevant miniminds. Clearly, individual decisions vary widely depending on the preferences of these agents and the process used to reach the decision (instead of a non-cooperative game, it could be a cooperative game with majority vote, or a turn-taking rule).

In my 2013 work, which aimed to explain decisions related to sustainable development, I modeled two adults as a Self Agent and a Species Agent. The Self

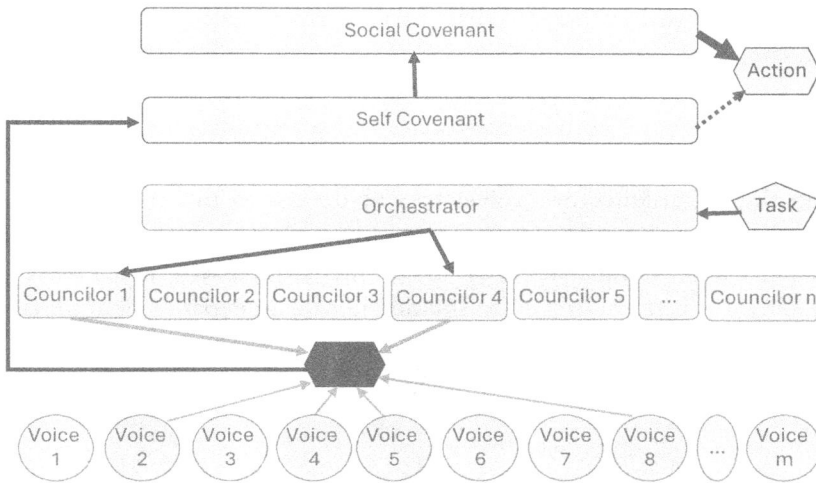

FIGURE 10.1   Architecture G for tDI.

Agent's goal is to ensure the maximum utilities of the individual, irrespective of its effect on others, society, and the species. The Species Agent, on the other hand, aims to ensure the individual serves the needs of the species and fulfills its role in survival and reproduction, irrespective of personal utility.

Similar to miniminds, these supervising agents (adults) may be innate (through genetics) or from life experience. External influences can shape us through supervising agents in three ways: seeding fresh agents, amplifying/suppressing existing ones, or modifying the process of how supervising agents reach a decision.

This game-theoretical framework forms the foundation of the tDI architecture I propose here: **Architecture G** (G refers to games) (Figure 10.1). There are five distinct components in Architecture G: **Voices, Councilors, Orchestrator, Self Covenant,** and **Social Covenant**. I discuss each of them in detail below and explain how they work together to make a decision. This architecture is designed to closely mimic how the human mind operates. It is based on connectionist AI (neurological structure) with explicit structure, combined with some symbolic components.

## Voices

Voices are equivalent to the miniminds (children) in our biological mind I described in my previous work. The two fundamental dimensions for classifying voices are: (1) innate vs. acquired, and (2) whether they ultimately serve the needs of the individual or the species.

I do not have an exhaustive list of voices. Investigating and uncovering as comprehensive a list of voices as possible is essential. I also note that there is substantial heterogeneity across individuals in what specific subset of voices they have, both acquired ones and some innate voices (at least in strength) due to genetic differences.

In the tDI architecture, voices may be developed in a hybrid manner. For some fundamental voices (such as sex drive), it is effective to explicitly allocate a specific substructure of the model to represent such a voice. At the same time, the architecture should allocate an expandable number of empty substructures that can each be occupied by a unique voice during training, without specifying which specific voices they will be.

## Councilors

Councilors are equivalent to the supervising agents (adults) in our bio-logical mind I described in my previous work. There are many councilors. Similar to voices, councilors can be classified as either innate or acquired, and either serving the individual or the species. While I hypothesize the two most prominent councilor pairs are the efficiency–equity pair and the individual–species pair, there are other councilors, and they do not neces-sarily need to have a counterpart (as a pair).

The set of councilors is much smaller than the set of voices. I do not have an exhaustive list of councilors either, and identifying as many rel-evant councilors as possible is essential in designing tDI. I also note that there is some heterogeneity across individuals in what specific subset of councilors they have, not just acquired, but also some innate councilors due to genetic differences. The major difference, I suspect, is the strength of these councilors rather than whether they exist.

In the tDI architecture, councilors may also be developed in a hybrid manner. For some fundamental councilors (such as efficiency), it is effec-tive to explicitly allocate a specific substructure of the model to represent such a councilor. At the same time, the architecture should allocate an expandable number of empty substructures that can each be occupied by a unique councilor during training, without specifying which specific coun-cilors they will be.

## Orchestrator

Orchestrator is a component that I have not used in my previous work, but it is critical when attempting to build a complete digital mind like tDI. In short, the orchestrator is the entity responsible for selecting which councilors are called upon to make a decision when tDI is presented with a task. We can imagine the orchestrator as the entity determining the framework within which the decision is made.

The orchestrator has the power to select councilors in each situation; however, it has no influence over how these chosen councilors make their decisions. We could add additional flexibility to the architecture by allowing multiple orchestrators; however, I believe one orchestrator provides sufficient flexibility in tDI.

For a given situation, different humans' orchestrators may select different councilors even under otherwise identical conditions. In fact, there is a stochastic element in this process, such that even the same individual's orchestrator may select different councilors for the same situation. The corresponding orchestrator should occupy a central substructure in tDI, without specifying how it works *a priori*, and allow training to determine how it operates, including the stochastic aspect of its selection.

## Self Covenant

Self Covenant is a new component in the architecture that I have not previously proposed. Unlike the previous components (Voices, Councilors, the Orchestrator), it is constructed using a symbolic approach, with hard-coded rules. This ensures absolute transparency and trust in tDI.

Self Covenant is analogous to the constitution of a nation. Any decisions that come out of the tDI (through the interaction of the Orchestrator, Councilors, and Voices) must be compared to it, and only those not in violation of the Self Covenant can be implemented.

Self Covenant consists of absolute rules such as "do not date anyone under 20" and also includes conditional rules where the conditions can be judged unambiguously, such as "do not kill a human being unless that person is trying to kill you". A person can decide how many rules to include in their Self Covenant. Of course, this can be updated anytime at the sole discretion of the individual. The tDI itself could also propose rules to include based on its understanding of the individual, but the decision to include such rule or not will only be made by the individual.

The Self Covenant can be made public to other tDI or humans, if the individual chooses. Obviously, publicly disclosing one's Self Covenant generates much higher trust from other tDIs or humans. On the other hand, one may lose privacy and place their tDI at a slight disadvantage in interactions with others. I suggest this decision be left to each individual.

## Social Covenant

Similar to the Self Covenant, the Social Covenant is a new component as well, constructed using a symbolic approach with hard-coded rules. The content of the Social Covenant is determined by society, typically through a national government, and is publicly available to everyone. A specific tDI may decide whether to incorporate the Social Covenant into its framework. If it does, all decisions it makes must not violate the Social Covenant before implementation. In addition, it outranks any rules in the Self Covenant. In other words, any rules in the Self Covenant that violate the Social Covenant will not be upheld.

The inclusion of the Social Covenant is optional, and if adopted, a specific tDI may attain a Social Covenant Verified status and be labeled as such. Such a label would introduce additional transparency and increase trust. It is also possible that a government might mandate adherence to the Social Covenant.

## An Example of Decision Flow in tDI

The illustration of Architecture G (Figure 10.1) includes an example of decision flow. In this case, the orchestrator reacts to the initiation of a task by selecting two councilors (c1 and c4). Councilors 1 and 4 then evaluate the needs of the affected Voices (v2, v4, v5, v8) and formulate a tentative decision (as represented by the solid hexagon). The tentative decision is then forwarded to the Self Covenant to check for any potential violations. If the decision violates any rule in the Self Covenant, it will be stopped. If it does not, and there is no Social Covenant, it will be implemented (action). If the tDI contains a Social Covenant, a tentative decision that passes the Self Covenant will be further forwarded to the Social Covenant to check for any potential violations. Only decisions that also pass the Social Covenant will be implemented (action).

## Kill Switch in tDI Architecture

It may be useful to consider including a Kill Switch in the architecture, with two settings. The first setting allows the user to take their tDI out of operation, ranging from hibernation to full deletion, as they see fit. The second setting is automatic and will be triggered as soon as the human dies, in other words, the tDI terminates itself when the individual dies. This structure is the ultimate guarantee to ensure incentive alignment so that tDI will act in the best interest of its human self. This is especially critical as tDI becomes smarter and even attains consciousness in the future. However, these are controversial decisions from the perspective of DI ethics. If DI has gained life and liberty (Figure 1.1), is it moral to develop a tDI whose fate is sealed and determined by its human self? Regardless of whether we include such kill switch in the architecture, it is absolutely necessary to have a mechanism to fully align the interest of tDI with its human self.

## Additional Considerations in tDI Architecture

There are additional aspects that need to be incorporated into the architecture, but they have been extensively discussed in public domains, and I will not repeat them here.

# A COMPANION WORTH BUILDING

Designing a tDI is daunting. We are not simply building a system that answers questions or performs tasks, instead, we are shaping a digital companion that must understand us, wrestle with our contradictions, act in ways that honor who we are and who we strive to become, and be our guardian in the DI world. That's a tall order, especially when we ourselves often waver between conflicting values, uncertain desires, and changing priorities.

And yet, this is precisely why it's worth doing. A tDI is not meant to eliminate life's complexity. It is meant to stand with us as we confront it, to be a quiet presence that remembers what we said when we were clear-headed, to ask us the hard questions we might avoid, and to hold us accountable to the principles we once pledged when things were calm. When designed thoughtfully, our tDI can give us more than convenience or intelligence, it can give us clarity, consistency, and trust. In the years to come, as we entrust more of our lives to DI, the difference between a generic DI assistant and a true tDI may mean everything.

# THOUGHT EXPERIMENT: NOT JUST MORAL DILEMMA

In life, some decisions challenge our morality, while others reveal our shifting preferences without moral stakes. Both types expose our inner conflicts, values, and hidden decision-making mechanisms. This exercise invites you to reflect on both and gain a deeper appreciation of the challenges in developing a capable and trustworthy tDI that acts in the best interests of its human self.

Let's start with a few moral dilemma decisions, similar to the mother and wife dilemma described earlier. For each dilemma, please think carefully (and ideally write down):

- What would you choose? Or would you refuse to choose (similar to option 3 or option 4 in the mother and wife dilemma)?

- Which principles, beliefs, or emotions influenced your choice?

- Do you think your choice will depend on other factors? If yes, what are they and how are they going to affect your choice?

## Moral Dilemmas

- A runaway trolley is heading toward five people tied to the track. You stand next to a lever that can divert it onto another track, where only one person is tied. You must choose whether to do nothing, resulting in five deaths, or pull the lever, actively causing one death but saving five. This is the well-known trolley problem.

- You are hiding with a group from enemy soldiers who will kill everyone if discovered. A baby begins to cry loudly, risking the group's exposure. You face an impossible choice: smother the baby to keep the group hidden, sacrificing an innocent life, or let the baby cry, resulting in the deaths of everyone, including the baby.

- You are among a group of 20 people who are stranded without food, facing starvation. One option is to kill and eat one person, providing enough sustenance for the others to survive until rescue. The alternative is to refuse to kill, which preserves moral integrity but would lead to the death of everyone from starvation. Will you kill? Or will you permit another person to kill?

- You discover that your child has committed a serious crime. You must choose between reporting them to the authorities, upholding justice and societal responsibility but ruining their future, or protecting them by staying silent and covering it up, preserving your child but violating your moral and legal duty.

- You need to allocate a single dose of life-saving medication to either a young child, offering them a full life ahead, or an elderly scientist who has made substantial contributions to society in the past.

Now please evaluate a second set of situations, where no moral challenge is involved. Instead, the indecision comes from our fluid preferences. For each situation, please think carefully (and ideally write down):

- Recall the last three times you made this decision (skip a situation if it's not applicable to you).

- What did you choose each time, and why?

- Was the choice driven by habit, mood, convenience, or principle?

**Fluid Preferences**

- You stand before the freezer, craving the creamy sweetness of ice cream. One part of you longs for its taste and the pleasure it brings, while another part warns of the health consequences such as excess sugar, fat, and guilt over breaking your dietary goals. You are also aware that the pleasure is short-lived and disappears as soon as you swallow it.

- Each morning, you face a small but nagging choice, take the elevator, arriving quickly and effortlessly at your 4th floor office, or climb the stairs, gaining a brief moment of exercise and health benefit but taking more time and arriving slightly out of breath.

- You notice something your partner said or did that stung, such as a careless comment, a forgotten promise, or another small act that left you hurt. Now you face a familiar inner debate, do you bring it up, risking defensiveness, argument, or emotional distance but staying true to your feelings and nurturing open communication, or do you let it go, preserving harmony in the moment but quietly carrying the hurt, which might build up over time?

- You stand on a bustling street in an unfamiliar city, with countless dining options. Part of you feels excited to try a local specialty, immersing yourself in the authentic flavors of the place, creating a memory unique to this visit, but you are not certain whether you will like it. Another part of you, however, craves the comfort of familiar food, something you know you'll enjoy for sure, providing a sense of stability after a long, tiring day. Which dining option would you choose?

- You hear from a friend about a promising stock that has surged rapidly in recent weeks. Part of you feels the pull of excitement and urgency, not wanting to miss out on potential further gains, especially as your friend speaks confidently about its bright future. Yet another part of you warns yourself that buying now, after the surge, carries high risk of buying at the peak and losing money when the stock price drops. You wrestle between the fear of missing out and the caution of disciplined investing, knowing that either choice will shape how you feel about yourself as an investor.

After you complete this thought experiment, please consider how you would like your tDI to behave in each of these situations.

## REFERENCES

[1] Ding, Min. 2007. A theory of intraperson games. *Journal of Marketing.* 71(2):1–11.

[2] Ding, Min. 2014. *The Bubble Theory.* English ed. Cham: Springer. 泡泡理论——人类社会何去何从, 2014 (Chinese Edition), 2018 (updated edition with new content). Shanghai: Fudan University Press.

# CHAPTER 11

# Data Generation and Preservation for Tutelary Digital Intelligence

## MUSK'S 80K POSTS

Elon Musk joined Twitter (now X) in 2009 and had posted more than 80k times as of July 2025, often posting 10 times or more each day for his 222 million followers. Musk's posts mix seriousness and humor. They cover business updates, provocative statements, philosophical musings, and deeply personal struggles (such as health issues or loneliness). Here are some of his interesting posts:

Decision to sell almost all physical possessions, affirming his belief that physical possessions serve only to distract him from his pursuit:

I am selling almost all physical possessions. Will own no house.

*(11:10 PM · May 1, 2020)*

Followed by his comment a day later: *My gf @Grimezsz is mad at me*

Observation on the theme of most entertaining outcome is the most likely outcome. This reflects his humorous side while subtly reflecting his fascination with the idea that we might be in a simulation by advanced

DOI: 10.1201/9781003711131-14

civilizations (he also posted about this simulation idea directly several times). He posted several variations of this over the year:

> The most entertaining outcome is the most likely – my variant on Occam's Razor
>
> *(Nov 20, 2022)*

> The most entertaining outcome – as if we're in a soap opera – is the most likely
>
> *(Mar 17, 2024)*

Opinion on population collapse and its impact on civilizations, with many posts around this theme:

> Population collapse is 2nd biggest danger to civilization after AI imo
>
> *(9:53 AM July 15, 2020)*

Revelation of deeply personal health issues:

> I was first misdiagnosed at Stanford Hospital with viral meningitis, then again misdiagnosed at Sequoia. A visiting doc from San Jose General saw my charts & sent me to ICU immediately. I was ~36 hours from being unrecoverable. So, I take expert advice with a grain of salt …
>
> *(5:40 AM March 17, 2020)*

> I have serious concerns about SSRIs, as they tend to zombify people. Occasional use of Ketamine is a much better option, in my opinion. I have a prescription for when my brain chemistry sometimes goes super negative.
>
> *(11:14 AM August 5, 2023)*

Thoughts and behavior related to his work, including ones that are quite personal:

> Btw, just want to express a word of appreciation for the hard work of the Tesla Gigafactory team. Reason I camped on the roof was

because it was less time than driving to a hotel room in Reno. Production hell, ~8th circle ...

*(5:10 AM October 27, 2017)*

Tesla stock price is too high imo 11:11 PM May 1, 2020

Even with this small sample, it is clear that his posts are not filtered. Musk wrote whatever came to his mind at the time and often disregarded the consequence of such posts (the post on Tesla stock led to a major decline in stock price in minutes).

Such comprehensive and unfiltered posts over a long time period represent the ideal type of data to train one's tDI. While not everybody is willing to make their thoughts public through social media, it is not a stretch to make a few short observations about one's life each day as it happens, and record them in text, audio, or video for private consumption.

## THREE-PRONGED APPROACH TO PERSONAL DATA COLLECTION

As we stand at the threshold of a future where your tDI acts as an extension of your mind, embodying your values, and guiding your decisions, the actions you take today in preserving, curating, and managing your personal data will be critical in shaping how your future tDI behaves and evolves. I will not cover data topics already discussed extensively in public domains, such as data sovereignty and privacy. Instead, I discuss a three-pronged approach to collecting valuable personal data: Passive Capture, Active Logging, and Constructed Elicitation, with an emphasis on Constructed Elicitation.

### Prong 1: Passive Capture

This refers to collecting data that is automatically recorded from daily life, both online and offline. These online data are often referred to as your digital footprint, and they include but are not limited to:

- Social Media Interactions: Posts, comments, likes, and shares provide insights into your opinions, interests, and communication style.

- Financial Records: Transactions, budgets, and investment history from online accounts reflect your spending habits and economic priorities.

- Health and Fitness Data: Information from wearable devices and health apps can reveal patterns in your physical well-being and daily routines.

- Communication Logs: Emails, text messages, voice and video recordings capture your language use, emotional tone, conversational patterns, and facial expressions.

- Digital Media Consumption: The content you view, stream, or download informs your cultural tastes and intellectual pursuits.

While your digital footprint is automatically recorded, these data are often distributed across many apps, platforms, and devices. They may also be deleted by the firms that host them. It is thus critical to develop a central data depository to aggregate data from these diverse sources and preserve it forever. This dataset serves as the historical context for your future tDI, providing a rich record that reflects your behavior and choices over time.

The offline data include but are not limited to:

- Personal Communications: Handwritten letters and postcards, personal journals or diaries, greeting cards with personal messages.

- Photo, Audio, and Video: Film or printed photos with notes or dates, home videos.

- Legal and Government Records: Birth, marriage, and death certificates, passports and national ID documents, court records (e.g., divorce, custody, legal disputes), military service records, land ownership or deed records, tax filings (paper format), driver's license records, voting registration and history (paper).

- Educational Records: Diplomas and degrees, report cards and transcripts (paper), standardized test results (e.g., SAT, GRE), teacher or advisor evaluations, awards and certificates.

- Health and Medical Records: Paper prescriptions, vaccination cards, doctor's notes or referrals (printed), physical exam or lab result printouts, dental records.

- Employment and Professional Records: Employment contracts (paper), performance reviews (paper), pay stubs or printed payroll records, business cards exchanged.

- Financial and Asset Records: Bank statements mailed to home, loan or mortgage documents, insurance policies (paper copies), receipts for major purchases, tax documents.

- Travel and Experience Records: Boarding passes (paper), stamped visa pages in passports, travel brochures or itineraries, guestbooks signed at events or museums.

For offline data, the first step is to digitize these records before incorporating them into your central data depository.

Passive Capture is the easiest of the three prongs to implement, but it is rich in content and provides the foundation for future tDI training.

### Prong 2: Active Logging

This refers to intentionally recording actions, thoughts, or preferences that are not automatically tracked. The goal is to preserve otherwise internal experiences or behaviors that would be lost without user effort. During the 24 hours of a typical day, only a fraction of what we think or do is ever recorded. Just imagine a typical working day: you get up, pick out clothes to wear, drive to the office, have one meeting with your supervisor and two separate meetings with your direct reports, have lunch in the company cafeteria and talk to a few people who happen to sit next to you, then have one long team meeting with your colleagues, work on your computer, go home, talk to your spouse about the day and family, make and eat dinner, take a walk and talk to some neighbors you bump into, then come back and sleep. Put a camera on you (such as those integrated into eyeglasses or a pin) to record this entire day, and do this every day, would be infeasible due to data storage and privacy concerns. Nevertheless, this is no reason to go through your day without recording key moments. In addition to the primary external data (what actually happened), it is extremely important to record annotations on what happened that day, like adding a comment such as: "When John talked about his weekend camping trip during lunch, it reminded me of my childhood dream of visiting all countries in the world ... maybe I should really start to make a plan now instead of waiting until I retire". A diary is a form of such recording.

Active Logging requires making an effort beyond normal routines and some level of technological support. Nevertheless, a few apps are already serving this purpose or could be easily adapted. BeReal is an app very popular among young people in the United States. Its users receive a daily notification, and they need to take simultaneous photos (and now short videos) from both the front and back cameras. Since the app randomly chooses a time to send the notice each day, and users must upload them within 2 minutes of receiving the notice, these snapshots provide a genuine glimpse into real life. Apps based on this concept could help people record their authentic lives, but without the requirement to share this data with friends. Firms like BiliBili in China, which allow viewers to add comments to specific moments of video, could be adapted for a user to annotate slices of their own life.

In addition, I recommend making a short 2–3 minutes video log each day to record your experiences, ideas, inner thoughts, preferences, emotional responses, and reflections. This is the opportunity to capture important moments from the day that have not been recorded in real time, and more importantly, to include any important thoughts you might have had, not necessarily in reaction to any specific event. Over time, this video log will become a key component of your digital DNA, offering deep insights into how you think and feel. It is important to use video recording, instead of writing, for this purpose, as it can capture facial expressions and subtle body movements in addition to how you express yourself through voice. Keep in mind the video can take up a lot of storage space quickly if you do it every day. This is why I recommend keeping it short. If storage is not a concern, 5–10 minutes per day would be better. Don't worry about whether you will have time to watch them all later; your tDI will be able to digest these data easily.

## Prong 3: Constructed Elicitation

This refers to designing new scenarios, either simulated or real, that provoke decisions, reactions, or reflections specifically to reveal your inner self as comprehensively as possible. The goal is to create purposeful stimuli that generate unique data for deeper insight into your values, reasoning, or identity, data that would otherwise remain hidden or only appear partially across multiple sources. It also includes direct rule elicitation.

Constructed Elicitation requires careful design and implementation, not just data collection. There are many aspects of an individual's mind that rarely have the opportunities to surface in daily life and, without deliberate elicitation, tDI would never capture them. This is the most difficult type of data to obtain, but absolutely essential. Constructed Elicitation aims to remedy these data gaps. This could be thought of as the equivalent of field tests for a product, exposing yourself to a wide range of situations in order to gain a full understanding of who you truly are. As in any field tests, Constructed Elicitation must be guided by theory so that you can be sure all aspects of your mind have been explored. I describe next the HiCope Framework that can be used to design simulated or real scenarios in Constructed Elicitation.

## CONSTRUCTED ELICITATION USING HICOPE FRAMEWORK

Constructed Elicitation is the critical third prong of data collection for tDI and provides a comprehensive and deeper understanding of a human's mind. In this section, I will first describe one theoretical framework called HiCope that can be used to guide Constructed Elicitation, followed by a brief discussion on explicit rule elicitation, and a more detailed discussion on how you can design simulated and real scenarios to reveal your innermost self, both guided by the HiCope Framework.

### The HiCope Framework

The HiCope Framework (Figure 11.1) is a systematic model I proposed in my book *Rethinking Chinese Cultural Identity* [1]. It was devised to capture and articulate the underlying elements that determine who an individual is. The acronym "HiCope" stands for four interrelated components: Human-I-Cosmos (HiC), Objectives (O), Protocols (P), and Experiences (E). I provide a brief overview of the framework here and encourage you to consult that book for more details when needed (specifically, Chapter 3 and Figure 3.1 in that book).

HiC represents the foundational dimension that encompasses how individuals perceive both themselves and the cosmos. This component is rooted in the perennial human quest for meaning. It addresses a series of existential questions that have intrigued philosophers, scientists, and

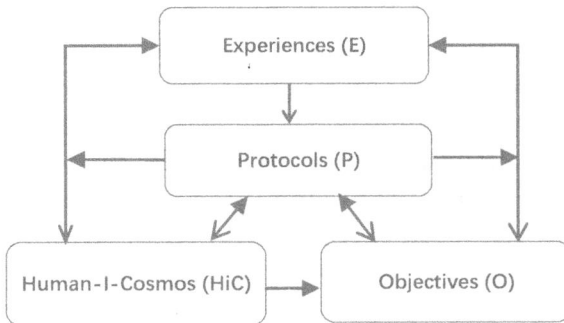

FIGURE 11.1   A Simple Illustration of the HiCope Framework.

spiritual thinkers alike: (1) Cosmic Origins and Purpose: What is the origin of the universe? What fundamental forces or principles govern its existence? What ultimate purpose (if any) underlies the cosmos? (2) Human Genesis and Destiny: How did humanity come into being? What is the role of the human race within the cosmic order? What is our collective destiny, and what factors might shape our future? (3) Personal Identity: Who am I? Beyond a simple acknowledgment of one's individual existence, this question invites us to examine one's inner nature, unique traits, and relation to the larger human community. At its core, HiC is an invitation to contemplate both the vast and the intimate. It asks us to consider the interplay between the grandeur of the universe and one's personal narrative. Some may approach these questions through empirical inquiry (using evidence, logic, and scientific reasoning), while others might rely on a belief-based or spiritual framework. Regardless of the approach, the answers we form influence our broader perspective on life, infusing day-to-day choices with a sense of purpose and connection.

Objectives (O) chart human aspirations. While understanding one's place in the cosmos establishes a context for existence, the next natural step is to define what one wishes to achieve in that context. The Objectives component captures the dreams, goals, and milestones that drive personal and collective progress. These objectives stem from the desires that include survival and reproduction while extending beyond them toward higher, more uniquely human aspirations. Objectives in the HiCope Framework are organized into two broad categories: Lifelong Objectives and Milestone Objectives. Lifelong objectives represent the overarching, enduring goals that a person aspires to fulfill over the course of one's existence. They are visionary and often abstract, serving as a north star to guide decisions and actions. These objectives encourage individuals to continually seek growth and align personal endeavors with a broader, meaningful purpose. Milestone Objectives complement lifelong goals and are more specific, actionable targets set over shorter time frames. These milestones serve as steppingstones that cumulatively lead toward the Lifelong Objective. They are concrete, measurable, and adjustable according to circumstances.

Protocols (P) establish guiding principles. Objectives must be pursued within a framework of consistent behaviors and practices. This is where the Protocols component comes into play. Protocols are the explicit and implicit rules, norms, and rituals that dictate the actions one should take or avoid in pursuit of objectives while remaining true to one's understanding of place in the cosmos. Protocols can be subdivided into several categories.

(1) Positive Rules are prescriptive directives that encourage good actions. They represent the "do's" of behavior and often encapsulate virtues such as kindness, honesty, integrity, and diligence. (2) Negative Rules, in contrast, are prohibitive guidelines that define boundaries by specifying what should be avoided. They are the "don'ts" that help prevent actions that could harm oneself or others. By clearly outlining what is unacceptable, negative rules serve to protect the integrity of both personal goals and cultural values. Many religions have negative rules. (3) Specific Events such as rites are structured ceremonies or practices that mark significant moments or transitions in life, reinforcing community bonds and personal commitment. (4) Reasoning encompasses the logical and ethical frameworks that justify protocols and guide actions. It is the internal dialogue or collective consensus that validates why specific practices are adopted, ensuring that protocols are not arbitrary but rather aligned with the overarching objectives and understanding of one's existence.

Experiences (E) are the lived reality. While the previous components are more reflective or prescriptive, experiences represent the empirical, tangible aspect of the human journey. They are the actual events, sensory perceptions, and internal reflections that constitute one's day-to-day life. Experiences provide the real-world feedback necessary to affirm or challenge one's understanding of the Human-I-Cosmos (HiC) and objectives (O). They allow a person to test protocols (P) against the unpredictability of life. For instance, a profound personal success or a challenging setback may prompt a re-evaluation of one's goals or lead to adjustments in the guiding rules. Over time, cumulative experiences help solidify an individual's identity, refining one's understanding of who one is and what one stands for. Experiences can be broadly classified into two categories. (1) Internal Experiences encompass the introspective aspects of life, the thoughts, emotions, and meditative insights that occur independently of external stimuli. They include moments of imagination, (day) dreaming, self-reflection, and internal dialogue. Internal experiences are critical for understanding the self and for the continual refinement of personal objectives. (2) External Experiences are sensory in nature, arising from interaction with the environment. They include everyday events and sensory inputs such as sights, sounds, and tastes, as well as interactions within social contexts and even virtual engagements.

At its core, the HiC determines the O. In turn, HiC and O determine the P. In addition, HiC and O also drive what E one will actively pursue, to the extent that is within one's control. P moderates how HiC and O influence E. A person's HiCope is not static. E provides strong feedback to HiC,

O, and P that may lead to their revision. In addition, the process of formulating P may also lead to adjustments in HiC and O, though its feedback effect is weaker than that of E.

### Direct Rule Elicitation

The first thing you should do is to use your HiC, O, and, to some extent, P to construct a personal manifesto as the blueprint for your tDI. This document outlines your personal values, long-term goals, ethical priorities, and the rules by which you wish to live. Over time, as you evolve, this manifesto should be revisited and refined, ensuring that your digital guardian remains in tune with your ever-changing identity. This manifesto serves as the core of the Self Covenant by providing explicitly coded rules, and it can also be used as part of the data to train other components of tDI. In addition, direct rule elicitation can help identify councilors, their nature and mode of operation, and, to some extent, a subset of voices.

### Simulated Scenarios

Simulated Scenarios can be considered as war games. The most informative simulated scenarios are those that take a long time to resolve, which typically means the relevant councilors are having a hard time reaching a conclusion. Such simulated scenarios provide only a glimpse into your councilors and voices, but they are still a useful starting point in developing your tDI.

In fact, you can use simulated scenarios to capture your decisions in any situation, even those that you are unlikely to encounter in real life but that offer insights into your true self. For example, you can ask, what would you change in your life (work, family, friends, etc.) if someone gave you $100m or $1b? In addition to using thought experiments in these simulated scenarios, it is possible to conduct such simulations in digital reality (virtual reality or mixed reality) to elicit a more realistic reaction from yourself. It is also valuable for training tDI to capture the thought process leading to each decision, not just the decision itself. As the space of such simulated scenarios is effectively infinite, it is helpful to follow the HiCope Framework to identify the most informative scenarios.

While direct rule elicitation and simulated scenarios offer tools for obtaining data on any possible aspects, these data are hypothetical and will likely contain substantial hypothetical bias. Hypothetical bias refers to the difference between what people do in a hypothetical situation and what they actually do when the situation is real. The exception to this is the rules that the individual explicitly encodes in their tDI, mainly those in Self Covenant.

Since these rules carry real and direct consequences, they are unlikely to contain hypothetical bias. I have studied hypothetical bias in decision-making for many years. In hypothetical situations, people seldom attempt to lie intentionally, as lying is cognitively costly and introduces dissonance that makes the individual uncomfortable. Instead, people in hypothetical situations simply provide an answer that is easy to generate (without thinking hard), such as what others do in the same situation, or what is expected by society. For example, in one of my studies [2], I found people were willing to pay much more for an extended warranty for an iPod in a hypothetical situation than when buying it for real. They were also much more adventurous and risk-seeking in hypothetical situations. Thus, you must balance the richness of information with likely hypothetical bias in simulated scenarios.

Real Scenarios

The antidote to hypothetical bias is real scenarios, where individuals actually live through the situation and their preferences and behaviors are recorded. This is the quintessential field test, and the goal is to throw yourself into many challenging real situations to reveal your true colors, sometimes in ways not even recognized by you. Unlike Simulated Scenarios, the number and nature of Real Scenarios are greatly constrained by cost and time. A balance between direct rule elicitation, simulated scenarios, and real scenarios is therefore necessary to complete the Constructed Elicitation process for tDI.

We can use the E component in the HiCope Framework, and its relationship with HiC, O, and P, to guide the design of low-cost, high-signal real scenarios. The most important design criterion is to ensure that scenarios activate elements of HiC, O, and/or P so the resulting data reveal more fundamental aspects of yourself, which are especially useful for constructing tDI. In addition, one should engineer a genuine trade-off such that every scenario forces you to give up one valued thing to gain another; otherwise, no deep insights can be uncovered. Ideally, the scenarios should cover as many domains as possible, but at a minimum they should include major life domains such as health, safety, money, and relationships (family and friends). You should also preserve the most informative data, for example, by using a neutral third party (human or camera) to capture high-fidelity records that reduce self-report bias and provide richer context for later annotation; and by conducting a self-debrief immediately after each scenario to record feelings, surprises, reasoning, and process. This reflection often reveals hidden councilors and voices, and one may even note directly which Voices were likely activated, which Councilors were salient, and any Self-Covenant or Social-Covenant constraints triggered.

## THE ONE SURE THING YOU COULD NOT AFFORD TO SKIP

It is hard to predict how the future will turn out, including how DI will evolve. However, there is one sure thing you can do today that will remain valuable no matter how the future unfolds. This one sure thing is generating and preserving data every day that captures who you are as a person.

Your future tDI can only be as good as the raw material you give it. A short daily video, a quick annotation after a tough meeting, or a well-designed weekend challenge that tests a value you claim to hold is the training fuel that will let a digital version of you reason, negotiate, and watch your blind spots when the stakes are high. Treat the habit of recording and generating data as you would exercise or saving money: small, regular deposits compound quickly. Start now, start small, and keep going. Ten years from now, you will either have a sparse record that forces your tDI to guess, or a rich timeline that lets it act with confidence on your behalf.

## THOUGHT EXPERIMENT: WILL YOU SPILL THE BEANS?

Everybody seems to agree that we all have skeletons in our closet, although few people are willing to tell their closest friends what specific skeletons lie in their closet. I often use this observation to illustrate the complexity of human beings (myself included). For example, I have thoughts I do not share with anyone because they would scare people.

Let's do a thought experiment and see whether you have any specific thoughts or information about yourself that you will be unlikely to share with anyone. I have organized 20 categories into 4 broad types: Doubts, Thoughts, Opinions, and Behaviors. Please read each category carefully, and ask yourself the following questions:

- Do you have anything in this category?

- If yes, will you tell anyone (knowing you will receive a reaction, and risk having it leaked to others)?

- If yes, will you incorporate this information as training data for your tDI (knowing tDI will remember it and act accordingly later)?

Here are the 20 categories:
Doubts:

- Insecurity About Identity: deep doubts or confusion about who you really are, morally, intellectually, or emotionally.

- Spiritual Doubts: conflicted feelings about your faith or the meaning of existence.

- Existential Fears: raw fear of death, meaninglessness, or never being truly known by others.

Thoughts:

- Secret Desires: fantasies or wishes you have never acted on, including romantic, sexual, violent, or even bizarre.

- Darkest Impulses: split-second urges you would never act on but that frightened you by appearing.

- Taboo Thoughts: culturally or socially unacceptable thoughts you have never dared to say aloud.

- Imagined Revenge: fantasies of retaliation or control over those who wronged you.

- Unfulfilled Cravings for Recognition: secret desires to be recognized for credit you believe you deserve.

- Romantic Confessions: love for someone you never told or still harbor feelings for despite circumstances.

Opinions:

- Unspoken Judgments: harsh thoughts about people you love or admire, including family, friends, or colleagues.

- Bitter Resentments: long-held anger or bitterness about people, organizations, or issues you hide under a smile.

- Biases: stereotypes, prejudices, or discriminatory thoughts you quietly hold.

Behaviors:

- Private Emotional Crises: episodes of breakdowns, panic attacks, or suicidal ideation that you have hidden from everyone.

- Secret Regrets: major life choices you regret but cannot undo, such as relationships, careers, or betrayals.

- Shameful Moments: incidents from your past that evoke deep shame, even if no one else knows about them.

- Hidden Addictions or Compulsions: hidden addictive behaviors you feel you can control, such as food, pornography, substances, or spending.

- Past Harm Done: things you have done that hurt others but were never acknowledged or discovered.

- Dishonest Acts: lies you have told (personal or professional) that still weigh on your conscience.

- Hypocrisies: actions that directly contradict your stated values or public image.

Now reflect on your responses, and ask yourself:

- Are you worried that your future tDI will make wrong inferences about who you are if it is told the complete truth?

- Do you think withholding such information will cause your tDI to make suboptimal, even biased, decisions for you?

## REFERENCES

[1] Ding, Min. 2019. *Rethinking Chinese Cultural Identity: "The Hualish" as an Innovative Concept*. Singapore: Springer.
[2] Ding, Min. 2007. An incentive-aligned mechanism for conjoint analysis. *Journal of Marketing Research*. 44(2):214–223.

# CHAPTER 12

# Thriving with Tutelary Digital Intelligence

## TANG SHEN AND WUKONG

*Journey to the West* [1] is one of the most famous classical novels in Chinese literature. It tells the story of a Buddhist monk, Tang Shen, who travels to India to retrieve sacred scriptures, accompanied by the Monkey King, Sun Wukong. Wukong was assigned to protect Tang Shen by the Bodhisattva Guanyin, who recognized that while Tang Shen had the motivation and moral integrity for the mission, he lacked the practical skills needed to survive the journey on his own.

Tang Shen is sincere, learned, and committed to the spiritual purpose of the journey. But he is also overly trusting and often blind to danger. Wukong, in contrast, is quick to act and unapologetically blunt, but he sees through deception instantly and doesn't hesitate to do what is needed. One such story in the book is "Three Attacks on the White Bone Spirit". The White Bone Demon (Bai Gu Jing) attempts to capture Tang Shen by disguising herself three times, first as a young maiden, then as an elderly woman searching for her daughter, and finally as an old man awaiting his family. Each time, Sun Wukong sees through the deception and kills the demon's false form. Tang Shen, however, is unable to recognize the monster and believes Wukong has murdered innocent people, grows increasingly furious and eventually expels Wukong (who, fortunately, returns later to save Tang Shen from another danger).

DOI: 10.1201/9781003711131-15

Tang Shen gave the mission its purpose and direction, but it was Wukong's ability to spot danger and neutralize threats, often before Tang Shen even realized there was a problem, that kept the journey from ending prematurely. Tang Shen did not always understand Wukong's intentions at the time and often questioned his methods. But in the end, it was this pairing of purpose with practical judgment and capability that made it possible for Tang Shen to complete his mission successfully.

With tDI, every one of us will have our own Sun Wukong.

## GOLDFISH, DOG, CHIMP, AND DRAGON

There is a famous Russian proverb that says, "Trust but Verify", popularized in the West by Ronald Reagan during his presidency. In an infinitely repeated game (as described in game theory), taking trusting and cooperative actions in the early stages of interaction leads to better outcomes for all parties involved over the long term, as long as the actions are observable and punishment for deviations is severe and enforceable.

In our relationship with tDI, and even with pre-tDI tools, you must adopt the same attitude. These tools can interact with humans in highly persuasive and personalized ways, projecting an image of superior expertise on any topic regardless whether they have it or not (when was the last time one of these tools told you "I don't know"?). As a result, they can provide invaluable assistance while also potentially leading to disastrous outcomes for their human users, intentionally or unintentionally.

The two essential dimensions of verification in working with tDI and pre-tDI are capability and alignment. I have drawn a simple two-dimensional diagram (Figure 12.1) with four animals to illustrate the relationship between humans and their tDI (or pre-tDI tools).

- When capability and alignment are both low, you can think of the tools as **Goldfish**. They are pleasant to look at and even play with (stirring the water, dropping a toy into the tank), but the goldfish has no idea who humans are (no alignment) and is not intelligent.

- When alignment is high while capability is still limited, you have **Dogs**. They have been human's best friends for thousands of years, with strong alignment and trust (with rare exceptions). They are clearly more capable than goldfish, but their intelligence remains limited.

- When you get to **Chimpanzees**, they are highly intelligent and capable, but with much lower alignment with humans compared to dogs.

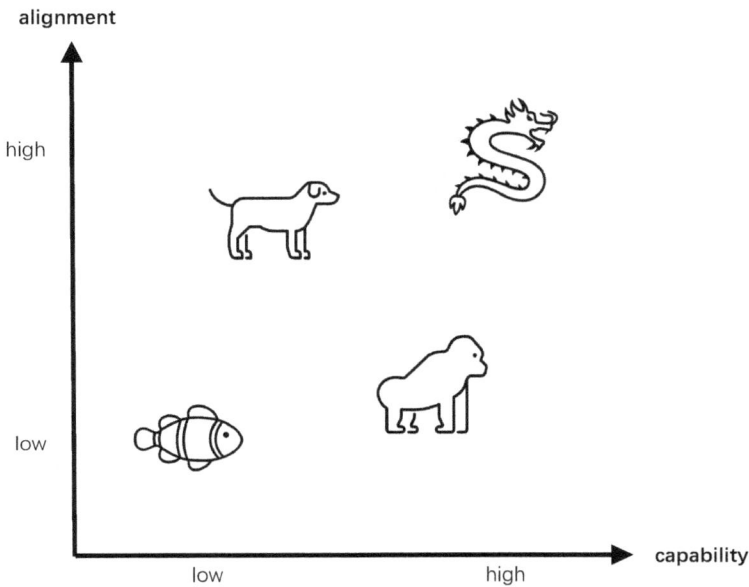

FIGURE 12.1   Goldfish, Dog, Chimp, and Dragon.

They may form close relationships with human caretakers, as seen in wildlife reserves, but you cannot know exactly what they have in mind. Their behavior is unpredictable, and they could easily turn against you if they choose.

- Finally, you have **Dragons**. These mythical creatures, described in many cultures, are vastly more powerful than humans. In East Asian traditions, dragons are protectors of royal dynasties. Like Wukong, they act in the best interests of their protectees in mind.

One thing you must avoid is mistaking one animal for another. This can be dangerous in the wild, and it could be even worse in dealing with tDI and pre-tDI tools. In the next section, I expand from this discussion on verifying capability and alignment and provide a comprehensive process for humans to assess and implement their relationship with their tDI (or any pre-tDI tools).

## PORTFOLIO OF AGENCY

It should be evident that it is foolhardy to give tDI (or pre-tDI tools) the same level of delegation for all tasks in your lives. In other words, you need to give different levels of agency (the ability to choose which actions

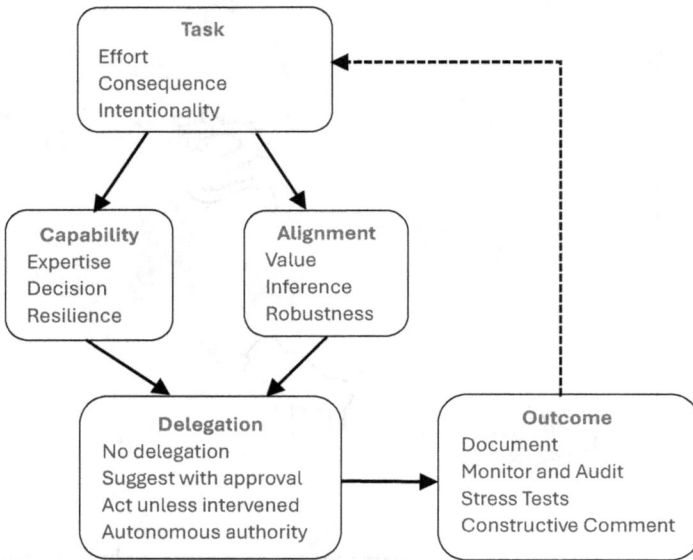

FIGURE 12.2   Constructing a Portfolio of Agency.

to take and then take the actions) across different tasks and make them conditional on the state of the tDI (or pre-tDI tools) for that particular task (consumption, financial, medical, relationship, etc.). This is why I call this a Portfolio of Agency. I describe next how to construct such a portfolio, through assessments of Task, Capability, and Alignment, followed by decisions on Delegation, and ongoing evaluation and learning through Outcome (Figure 12.2).

Task Assessment

First, you need to assess the nature of each task to be delegated to tDI (or pre-tDI tools). There are three major dimensions that must be evaluated: effort, consequence, and intentionality.

**Effort** refers to the effort required if you complete the task yourself. This includes both the expertise needed (or that must be acquired) and the cost in time and energy required to complete one instance of the task, multiplied by how frequently such tasks occur in your life.

**Consequence** refers to the impact of the outcome from a completed task. Choosing lunch is of low consequence, while choosing which house to buy is of high consequence. You should also consider whether the consequence is (partially) reversible. Clothing choices can be easily reversed, but medical decisions are much harder to undo.

**Intentionality** is the third important dimension. It reflects how important it is for you to be directly involved in the decision-making process, regardless of decision quality. For example, you could either pick a gift for a friend or delegate the task to your tDI. Even if the gifts are identical, your friend will likely be much more pleased if you personally selected it.

## Capability Assessment

Next, you need to assess the capability of a tDI (or pre-tDI tool) for each task to be delegated. The goal is to ascertain whether it is sufficiently capable of handling the task. There are three major dimensions that must be evaluated: expertise, decision, and resilience.

**Expertise** refers to whether the system has the correct and comprehensive grasp of all knowledge related to the task, and whether it can learn from feedback, recognize changing patterns, and update its knowledge base.

**Decision** refers to the system's ability to understand a relevant task, make inferences (even with incomplete information), generate a solution, and execute it. It must also be able to adapt to specific contexts or situational nuance.

**Resilience** refers to the system's ability to function in abnormal situations, including conflicting data or miscommunication. It also includes the capacity to resist manipulation by other tDI (pre-tDI tools) or humans.

## Alignment Assessment

Once you have a good understanding of a system's capability regarding a specific task, you need to assess whether it will behave in your best interest for that task. This assessment rests on three dimensions: value, inference, and robustness.

**Value** refers to whether the tDI (or pre-tDI) has a value system different from you, it should not. At a minimum, its values should closely mirror yours for the task at hand.

**Inference** refers to the system's ability to correctly infer your intentions. A system might be trained to perform a task flawlessly, yet still be misaligned if it misunderstands what you actually want. Empathy is a powerful skill that some humans practice more effectively than others. tDI (or pre-tDI) will need to have a sufficient degree of digital empathy to be aligned with you. They must also be able to understand and act when there are conflicts in your own preferences.

**Robustness** includes both transparency and resistance to alignment breakdown. Transparency ensures trust in alignment and confidence in the decisions made by tDI. In addition, a system must attain high robustness so that neither its values nor its inferences collapse due to internal weaknesses or external interference. You can imagine that in the future, countless attempts may be made by other tDI to manipulate or redirect the loyalty of your tDI.

## Delegation Decision

Once you have a good understanding of the task, and the system's capability and alignment regarding that task, you can decide how much delegation is appropriate for that system regarding this task.

The default level is **No Delegation**. You will seek information and suggestions from tDI (pre-tDI) systems, even brainstorm with them, but you will not rely on them to make the decision itself. This stage is only a step above using a search engine to refine your own thinking.

When appropriate, you can give your tDI (or pre-tDI) more agency and ask it to provide a well-reasoned recommendation. At this stage, you review each recommendation and manually approve it before execution. This is the **Suggest with Approval** level. For example, a tDI (pre-tDI system) will send a lunch choice recommendation to you through email at least two hours before noon. It will place the order only if it receives affirmative confirmation from you; otherwise, it will do nothing.

The next level up is called **Act Unless Intervened**. You can think of live television, where broadcasters insert a short delay to censor inappropriate content. Under Act Unless Intervened, the tDI (pre-tDI if relevant) formulates and executes a decision unless you intervene within a predefined time frame. In the lunch choice task, a tDI (pre-tDI system) with this level of agency will make a lunch choice, wait for a set period (e.g., 30 minutes), and place the order if it receives no response from you.

Finally, you could endow a tDI (pre-tDI) system with full authority for a specific type of task. Under **Autonomous Authority**, the system acts independently without your involvement. In the lunch choice example, it will simply order your lunch without contacting you first.

These levels are not fixed, they can be dynamically adjusted through escalation rules that specify when the system should seek greater human involvement.

## Outcome Assessment

The last component of the framework is Outcome Assessment. In addition to **Documenting** and sharing the outcomes and your evaluations of these outcomes with the tDI (pre-tDI) tool, it is also important to conduct regular audits, perform stress tests, and give constructive feedback to help the tDI (pre-tDI) improve.

**Monitor and Audit** involves detailed assessments of past decisions across all tasks a tDI (pre-tDI) has undertaken. This includes analyzing each task, the process a tDI (pre-tDI) used to reach its conclusion, and whether there is behavioral drift or other anomalies.

It is also helpful to conduct **Stress Tests** from time to time. In these cases, you assign unusual, ambiguous, or conflicting tasks to the tDI (pre-tDI) and observe how it responds.

Finally, it is absolutely critical to provide **Constructive Comment** to the tDI (pre-tDI tools). These may come from regular usage, audits, and stress tests, as well as any practical suggestions for improvement. Constructive comments close the feedback loop and feed back into earlier stages of assessment and decision-making.

## USE PRE-TDI TOOLS NOW

It would be unwise to wait any longer before you use pre-tDI tools to help you navigate your life. These tools are becoming more capable every month, and delaying their use will put you at a disadvantage. Moreover, getting used to them now will ease the eventual transition to working with a personal tDI.

Pre-tDI tools are generic AI assistants with fast-improving usefulness. They are advancing rapidly, though they still have a long way (or a short distance, if you ask the optimists) to go before they match or surpass the best human experts. In addition, they are not trained to think and behave in a particular individual's mindset and interest. Their guidance is typically generic and not personal (though this can be partially remedied through prompts), and they are not connected to your life story, emotional profile, or deepest aspirations, regardless of how carefully you craft your prompt.

Despite these limitations, pre-tDI digital assistants are already influencing many aspects of society. The most obvious area is work and productivity, which I will not revisit here (see Part II). Less obvious but equally profound, they are helping people navigate other areas of life.

In commerce, we are beginning to see real changes in how consumers make decisions and how businesses must respond. Personalized recommendation systems powered by pre-tDI assistants, when used thoughtfully, can already help individuals align purchases with their values. They can filter for environmentally responsible products, account for long-term costs, flag manipulative advertising, or curb impulsive spending in favor of intentional choices. For example, they can detect business tactics that exploit human cognitive biases (such as pricing a product at $9.99 to make it seem closer to $9 than $10). Such tricks become meaningless once a pre-tDI assistant filters the choice. At a more complex level, they may analyze why a Gucci bag is priced at $10,000, breaking down costs and margins, and advise whether it is worth buying compared to a $1,000 bag from a regional Italian brand. A consumer can no longer afford to shop without such assistance. On the business side, this requires adapting marketing strategies from appealing to human psychology with limited cognitive capacity toward meeting the scrutiny of logic-driven intermediaries with perfect memory of past purchases and usage. Brands that prioritize transparency, ethical practices, trust, and long-term value will thrive in a marketplace increasingly shaped by pre-tDI assistants acting on behalf of discerning consumers.

Pre-tDI assistants are also helping humans with their personal lives, social lives, and broader citizenship. Many people already use them as counselors or psychologists for aspects of daily life. In addition, many turn to them first when faced with a health issue. There is even a post on X showing a photo of an emergency room doctor typing a patient's symptoms into a ChatGPT interface to ask for a diagnosis. Although the authenticity of the post cannot be fully verified, some prominent medical doctors now argue it is negligent not to consult such tools before making a diagnosis or treatment plan. Of course, they should only be used for gathering information or suggestions with human approval (the first two levels of delegation in our Portfolio of Agency). If doctors are using them, we can imagine how many individuals are using them at home for self-diagnosis or as a second opinion. They can also provide recommendations on managing social interactions, family relationships, or even group dynamics. These tools are useful for simulating how others might interact in settings such as interviews, dating, or social gatherings. Many undergraduates I taught have found interview simulations with pre-tDI assistants to be one of the most valuable AI applications. They have also been applied to analyzing political discourse, an especially valuable tool given today's flood of information and disinformation, helping people make civic choices, including voting.

Since pre-tDI assistants are not personalized to think, act, and safeguard a specific individual, it is critical to become proficient in communicating with them effectively. In the early days of GenAI, there was much hype about prompt engineering. I prefer to call it communication because prompting implies reactiveness. I characterize pre-tDI tools as smart but lazy, and the way you communicate with them makes all the difference. They have vast knowledge and expertise, yet they are trained to produce responses that sound good enough, indistinguishable from human ones, but not necessarily the best possible answer. As a result, it falls on you to push and guide them into delivering exactly what is needed. There is a fast-growing knowledge base on how to improve their responses, including asking them to take on the persona of someone whose data is richly represented in training (e.g., "act as if you were Steve Jobs"). Fine-tuning a pre-tDI assistant to create a digital twin is an intermediate step toward tDI. I encourage you to become proficient in communicating with pre-tDI assistants and to do so as soon as possible.

## START WITH THREE HABITS

Following what I discussed in the previous section, I suggest you start by developing three habits of working with pre-tDI assistants, to benefit from their current capabilities while preparing for the eventual arrival of DI and your own tDI. Note that all three habits assume the first level of delegation, with the second level appropriate only for certain tasks, given their current limits in capability and alignment. I also recommend using multiple pre-tDI assistants by giving them the same instructions, so you can cross-check responses, identify consensus, and detect hallucinations.

Habit One: Before you make any major purchase, defined as purchase that costs more than a set threshold, holds significant personal value, or is the kind of decision you sometimes regret later, please consult your pre-tDI assistants. First, ask them to evaluate information such as ads, social media posts, PR campaigns, and customer reviews, separating fact from opinion and flagging bias or misleading claims. Then, share your values (short- and long-term), preferences, and past purchase experiences, along with your reason for considering the purchase. Ask them to conduct deep research and identify the options that best serve your objectives. Only after these steps should you make a decision.

Habit Two: Anytime you encounter a new health issue, instead of randomly searching online or ignoring it, clearly describe your situation to pre-tDI assistants. Ask them to suggest possible explanations and next steps, or to help you prepare to talk to a professional. For example, I once uploaded a photo of a rusty nail and my bleeding finger, explained my situation, and asked for advice. Based on their responses, I decided to go to a local drug store immediately for a tetanus shot rather than wait for a doctor's appointment the next day.

Habit Three: When you face a tricky situation, either at work or in personal life, where you are unsure how to respond, talk it through with pre-tDI assistants, giving them enough context. You don't need a perfect answer and should not follow their guidance blindly. Still, their perspectives can help you pause, reflect, and choose a better response.

Cultivate these habits, reflect on their outputs, and fine-tune your collaboration with these pre-tDI assistants. Once you feel comfortable about these three usage cases, you should consider using pre-tDI assistants in additional situations.

## THOUGHT EXPERIMENT: THE DEVOTED CEO OR SCIENTIST

Imagine yourself as a CEO or a scientist completely absorbed by your work. Every waking hour that is not directly related to your core mission feels like a distraction. You care deeply about outcomes that affect your health, family, comfort, and long-term wellbeing, but you have little desire to spend time or energy on making those decisions. You would rather delegate them entirely.

Now suppose you have someone you trust deeply, a long-time assistant, a spouse, or even a dedicated chief-of-staff. They know your preferences, priorities, and constraints. They have sound judgment and are willing to take full responsibility. You want to hand over the decision-making authority to them in as many areas of your life as you feel comfortable, freeing yourself to focus on your mission.

For this thought experiment, consider the following 20 categories of decisions. For each one, ask yourself:

- Who would you feel comfortable delegating this to, if anyone? (A specific person or role, such as spouse, assistant, friend, expert, or no one at all.)

- What makes you trust that person? Is it shared values, domain expertise, track record, emotional closeness?

- Would you delegate this temporarily or permanently?

- Would you still delegate if the outcome were irreversible or long term?

- If the decision went wrong, would you blame yourself or them?

Twenty categories of decisions

- What to eat for lunch or dinner
- Which hotel to stay
- Selecting and booking flights, trains
- What to wear to work today
- Managing your calendar (meetings, breaks, travel days)
- Which birthday gifts to send to friends and family
- What books to read outside work
- What phone or laptop to upgrade to
- Home decor and furniture purchases
- Which social engagements to accept or decline
- Which school to send your child to
- What diet or exercise routine to follow
- Where to live (city or neighborhood)
- When and where to take a vacation
- Which healthcare provider or insurance plan to choose
- Which politicians to support
- How to handle conflicts with a colleague or board member
- When to sell stock or make large investments
- Whether to hire or fire a close team member
- Whether and when to retire or step down

Once you have reflected on all 20 categories, look across your responses and identify common themes.

## REFERENCE

[1] Wu, Cheng'En. 16**th** century. *Journey to the West* 《西游记》.

# PART IV

## Seeking Vanguards for a Post-2045 World

W HEN I SHARE THE core ideas of this book with colleagues and executives, among others, I rarely hear them dismissed as outlandish. Instead, people usually pause and reflect on what their own lives could look like if this future of abundance, fairness, and peace becomes a reality. I remember one such conversation over lunch at Goethe University in Frankfurt. A colleague, one of their star professors, paused, reflected, and then said, "I could still play my guitar". Part IV is about finding your own guitar to play.

The chapters in this section are meant to serve as a guide to this discovery. They briefly explore eight pursuits that will define a meaningful life for *Homo lucidus* after 2045. Each of these eight pursuits captures a unique orientation of human aspiration and purpose in Lucidus Society, reflecting both our distinct identities and our collective quest for meaning. These eight pursuits are identified using the Enlightened Needs (EN) framework (Chapter 3) and the HiCope (Human-I-Cosmos, Objectives, Protocols, and Experiences) framework (Chapter 11), and are empirically validated through a systematic review of vanguards for each pursuit.

The pioneers of these pursuits, our vanguards of a post-2045 world, are not distant figures from a science fiction story. They are already living among us, people whose deep purpose already aligns with the future. Your goal is not simply to read about them, it is to seek them out, to learn from their approach to life, and to try out their pursuits in your own daily life. This will help you understand where your energy naturally flows, what

DOI: 10.1201/9781003711131-16

compels you, and what feels worth your time. As a result, you can best realign your current life for the future.

This exploration will also enhance the topics we discussed in Part II, from preparing your body and mind (Chapter 5) to understanding your human relationships and network (Chapter 6), your learning (Chapter 7), and your vocation (Chapter 8). What you choose to do now that aligns with a future pursuit will also provide your tDI with data to help it understand and support you better (Part III, Chapter 11).

We will first dive into the four types of Inner Pursuits, those that define a meaningful life through inward reflection, focused on things that could be done independent of others. They include the Hedonist, Aesthete, Inquisitive, and Cosmologist (Chapter 13). We will then explore the four types of Outer Pursuits, those that find meaning in outward-facing engagements, including the Connector, Culturist, Anthroguard, and Conservationist (Chapter 14). As you read Chapters 13 and 14, ask yourself which types of Lucidus Pursuit you feel drawn to, whether you know anyone who fits the descriptions, and whether you might want to become a vanguard in one of them. Finally, Chapter 15 will ask you to envision yourself and work to enable a personal future that you desire. You will then write a Future History of your life. This final thought experiment is designed to make you think deeply about the pursuits in a post-2045 world, plan out your own place in Lucidus Society, and take actions now.

# CHAPTER 13

# The Inner Pursuits – Hedonist, Aesthete, Inquisitive, and Cosmologist

THIS CHAPTER EXPLORES FOUR fundamental pursuits that define a meaningful life by looking inward, toward personal experience, intellectual exploration, and curiosity. They are the Hedonist, who seeks fulfillment through sensory and spiritual enjoyment; the Aesthete, who finds meaning in creating and celebrating human creativity and pushing the boundaries of expression; the Inquisitive, who is driven by an unyielding quest to understand the world; and the Cosmologist, who engages with the universe's grand, timeless questions and profound philosophical inquiry, those that the most advanced DI may continue to struggle to explain. These are pursuits that find their meaning from an internal source, pursuits that, in theory, could be undertaken even if the individual were the only living person left in the world. These four types of pursuits are represented as one arm of the Lucidus Pursuits (Figure 13.1), with the order roughly representing the scale of pursuit, from the individual (Hedonist) to the universe (Cosmologist).

For each of these pursuits, you will be introduced to a vanguard who embodies its spirit, serving as a real-world example to help you recognize

DOI: 10.1201/9781003711131-17

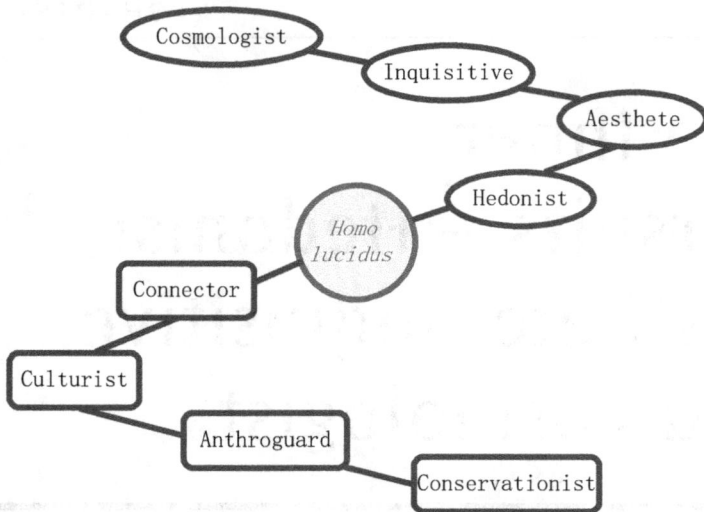

FIGURE 13.1   Lucidus Pursuits.

these pursuits in the world around you. Each vanguard's story is followed by an exploration of the pursuit's core philosophy and guiding principles. These examples are more than just stories; they are tangible guides to living a life of purpose, offering a framework for you to understand your own inner motivations. As you read, consider how these pursuits resonate with you and be ready to challenge their premise through the thought experiment that concludes the chapter.

## HEDONISTS

"The Best Climber Is the One Having the Most Fun."

Alex Lowe (1958–1999) was widely regarded as the strongest mountaineer of his era. Though his peers nicknamed him "the Lung with Legs" for his incredible stamina and numerous climbing accomplishments [1], his pursuit was never about fame or accolades. For Alex, a life well lived was one rich with raw, unfiltered experience. He viewed the world as an expansive playground where natural beauty and extreme conditions converged to evoke a sense of wonder. His lifelong goals were centered on pursuing the ultimate thrills of the outdoors, the feeling of stone under his hands, the sting of cold air on his skin, and the humility inspired by the mountains. This commitment to joy was his ultimate measure of success. He famously said, "the best climber is the one having the most fun" [1], a mantra that defined his approach to everything he did. In 1999, while attempting to be the first American to ski an 8,000-meter peak in Shishapangma, Tibet, Alex was tragically killed in an avalanche. But even in this final, audacious pursuit, he was doing what he loved most.

Alex Lowe was a vanguard Hedonist.

## Who Are the Hedonists

The individuals who embrace the Hedonist pursuit seek to maximize both physical pleasure and spiritual enjoyment by embracing new experiences. They frame their lives through a lens that values immediate, tangible sensations. For them, the purpose of existence is grounded in the sensory aspects of life, where stimulation and pleasure are essential components of a life well lived. This worldview shapes their approach to everything.

Their ultimate goal is to actively pursue pleasure and satisfaction. This is not about passive consumption; it is an unwavering commitment to seeking new physical and spiritual experiences. Their objectives are designed to secure a sustained, evolving state of fulfillment that adapts to their changing desires. This could involve everything from savoring gourmet food to engaging in immersive digital reality to scaling a mountain.

To achieve this, they craft a life around maximizing enjoyment while avoiding overindulgence. They embrace positive routines that encourage regular engagement with activities known to enhance well-being. Just as important, they adopt rules to safeguard their journey by avoiding stress, overconsumption, and similar excesses. This balanced approach ensures a life of sensory and spiritual abundance remains sustainable and deeply rewarding. They intentionally curate their decisions for the potential to contribute to a sustained state of enjoyment over time.

## AESTHETES

### Capturing Life's Quiet Beauty

Vivian Maier (1926–2009), a nanny by trade, lived for the quiet joy of capturing life's fleeting beauty through her camera lens, never seeking fame or fortune. After moving to Chicago in 1956, she roamed its streets, on her days off, snapping candid shots of strangers. Her images, over 150,000 in total, framed Chicago's gritty soul and human quirks. Vivian kept her work private, storing negatives in boxes, never developing many, as if the act of seeing was enough. In her later years, she switched to color film, capturing abstract shadows and vibrant urban details, still for herself alone. Her vast archive was discovered in 2008 when the content in her storage units were auctioned, which now has captivated the world, shown

in galleries and the documentary Finding Vivian Maier [2]. Her passion
was the art itself, each click of the shutter was a private celebration of life's
ordinary and yet extraordinary moments.

Vivian Maier was a vanguard Aesthetes.

## Who Are the Aesthetes

Aesthetes are driven by a deep appreciation for the human creative spirit
and a passion for artistic achievement. In a world where DI can generate
flawless creative work, they cherish expressive outputs that are unmistak-
ably human-made. They see human creativity not as a rival to DI but as
a distinct form of innovation rooted in subjective experience, personal
expression, and emotional resonance.

For Aesthetes, the universe is a vast canvas where human ingenuity
and imagination leave a unique mark. They believe our creative spirit is a
defining trait of our species and a critical part of the cosmos. This worldview leads them to champion authenticity, narrative complexity, and the
lived experience of creation.

Their ultimate goal is to pursue creative excellence and to preserve the
distinctly human dimension of art. Aesthetes set their sights on objectives
that highlight the inherent value of human expression shaped by personal
experience and deep emotion. They commit to generating and promoting
creative works that challenge conventional perceptions, cultivate cultural
narratives, and inspire future generations.

To achieve this, they adopt practices that encourage originality and
authenticity. They may set clear boundaries on how they use digital tools,
choosing to embrace instead the imperfections inherent in human-made
work. They seek out experiences that immerse them in the full spectrum of
human creativity, from attending live performances to watching a movie
crafted entirely by humans.

## INQUISITIVES

### Projecting Tomorrow

Trained formally as a biochemist, Isaac Asimov built a lifelong habit of
studying a wide range of disciplines, from physics and robotics to history,
literature, and even biblical studies. He was not content with surface-level
knowledge. He approached each field with methodical curiosity, striving to
understand both how things worked and what they might become. Over the
decades, he maintained a relentless pace of reading, thinking, and writing,
ultimately publishing over 500 books and tens of thousands of essays and

articles, covering nearly every major domain of human knowledge. In his fictions, he projected what future societies, technologies, and ethical dilemmas might look like based on plausible developments grounded in scientific reasoning and human psychology. His famous "Three Laws of Robotics", introduced in the 1940s [3], continue to shape how we think about machine intelligence and ethics. In nonfiction, his works aimed to make complex knowledge accessible and to chart the evolution of human understanding over time. He dedicated himself to becoming a clear and rigorous observer, someone who could grasp complex developments, think deeply about their consequences, and share those insights with others. He engaged deeply with the world's knowledge, looked ahead with intellectual honesty, and reflected critically on what the future might ask of us.

Isaac Asimov was a vanguard Inquisitive.

## Who Are the Inquisitives

Inquisitives are driven by an insatiable curiosity and a profound longing to understand the why behind phenomena, always seeking to anticipate what lies ahead. Recognizing that DI is destined to surpass BI, they do not compete with it. Instead, they center their lives on a deep appreciation for knowledge generated through DI and critical reflection on its implications.

They see the universe as a grand text that invites constant discovery, interpretation, and reflection. They admire the rich heritage of human scientific inquiry while also acknowledging the rapid rise of DI as an unprecedented source of insight. They perceive DI not as a threat, but as an opportunity to understand the complex tapestry of knowledge emerging in partnership between human and digital minds.

Their primary goal is deep intellectual discovery aimed at comprehending an unfolding future. They focus on engaging with and learning from the vast knowledge produced by the world, including that generated by DI, through attentive study and critical reflection. The ultimate aim is to participate in a vibrant, ongoing intellectual dialogue that enriches human understanding of the world and our place within it. In a way, they strive to be the best students of knowledge itself.

To achieve this, they adopt practices that emphasize intellectual curiosity and critical inquiry. They dedicate themselves to questioning assumptions, evaluating sources, integrating disparate information into coherent frameworks, and understanding implications of new knowledge. Their decision-making is informed by both empirical evidence and philosophical reflection, ensuring they remain open to new paradigms while anchored in rigorous analysis. This pursuit is sustained through self-study, scholarly discussions, and regular interactions with both human and digital mentors, using DI as a primary source of direct learning.

## COSMOLOGISTS

### Who Speaks for Earth?

Carl Sagan (1934–1996), a pioneering planetary scientist and cosmologist, devoted his life to exploring humanity's oldest and most profound questions. His work helped explain the greenhouse effect on Venus, mapped seasonal changes on Mars, and played a key role in NASA's Voyager, Viking, and Mariner missions. Yet what made Sagan extraordinary was his ability to unite discovery with existential wonder and inspire generations to think as the apex BI on Earth, to set aside divisions and focus on the fundamental questions that matter most. "Who speaks for Earth?" was the rallying cry he raised for our cosmic responsibility.

To Sagan, cosmology was an open-ended pursuit of meaning. Through *Cosmos: A Personal Voyage*, one of the most influential science series ever broadcasted, and in books like *Cosmos* [4] and *Pale Blue Dot* [5], Sagan invited millions to share in the awe of existence. He reminded us that we are "star stuff", not separate from the universe but born from it, and that our species could rise to the moment and try to understand our place in it, if we are willing to imagine, to ask, and to learn. He inspired generations of astronomers, physicists, writers, and curious minds to take up the cosmological quest in pursuit of ever-deeper questions.

Sagan was a vanguard Cosmologist.

### Who Are the Cosmologists

Cosmologists are defined by a relentless pursuit of the ultimate existential question: Why does the universe exist? They embrace the profound mystery at the heart of existence, fully aware that even with advanced DI they may never find a definitive answer. For them, the joy and satisfaction lie in the pursuit itself, through exploration, creative and philosophical inquiry, and the continual expansion of understanding.

Unlike the Inquisitives, Cosmologists push beyond what is known, often in ways that challenge the limits of DI itself. At the core of their worldview is a deep respect for the unknown, a recognition that the ultimate reason behind existence eludes even the most advanced forms of intelligence. Cosmologists are drawn to the scientific and metaphysical dimensions of our existence, viewing the universe as a vast, dynamic canvas meant to evoke introspection and awe.

The objectives for Cosmologists center on an unyielding dedication to the grand questions of existence. Their primary goal is to immerse themselves in cosmic inquiry, origins, purpose, and destiny, blending scientific exploration with philosophical depth. Their decision-making is informed by a commitment to intellectual autonomy and a deep-seated belief that the journey of inquiry is as significant as any eventual answer. They actively seek experiences that challenge and expand their understanding of the universe, finding joy in asking profound questions and exploring the unknown, knowing they are working on problems so fundamental that even DI cannot solve.

## THOUGHT EXPERIMENT: THE PURSUIT OF PERSONAL PURPOSE

Imagine you have the rare opportunity to sit across from the four vanguards introduced in this chapter, the Hedonist, the Aesthete, the Inquisitive, and the Cosmologist. Each has built a life around the pursuit of meaning drawn from within, choosing paths that reflect not wealth, power, or status, but their deepest sense of purpose. Yet you approach them not as an admirer, but as a skeptic armed with realism and even cynicism. Your role is to probe, to challenge, and to question whether their chosen pursuit was ever truly meaningful. Could their lives have been better spent chasing something else?

This thought experiment has three parts for each vanguard:

**The Challenge**. Formulate a sharp critique that cuts to the heart of their pursuit. Ask difficult questions, raise doubts, and highlight the limitations of their chosen path. Why should anyone value fleeting pleasures? Is private art that no one sees truly meaningful? Does relentless curiosity add up to more than words on a page? What good is contemplating cosmic mysteries that may never be solved? In short, make the strongest case for why their purpose was misguided or inconsequential.

**The Rebuttal**. Now imagine how each vanguard would respond in their own voice, drawing on their writings, speeches, or lived actions. What reasons would they offer to defend the worth of their life's work? How would Alex Lowe explain the joy of the climb or Vivian Maier explain the beauty in photographs? How might Isaac Asimov justify his insatiable curiosity or Carl Sagan justify the necessity of cosmic perspective? Let them answer your challenge point by point, stay true to their own perspectives, not generic responses.

**The Reflection.** Finally, step back and reflect on the exchange. What have you learned from pressing these vanguards and hearing their rebuttals? How does this deepen your understanding of why people commit themselves to such inner pursuits, even in the face of doubt or misunderstanding? More importantly, how does it help you understand why these four inner pursuits, the Hedonist, the Aesthete, the Inquisitive, and the Cosmologist, will remain vital in Lucidus Society?

Through this exercise, you are wrestling with the fundamental question of personal purpose, testing its strength by attacking it directly. What survives these challenges will give you a clearer sense of which pursuits resonate with you, and which may guide your own journey toward becoming a vanguard in an area of your choice.

## REFERENCES

[1] Poljak, Sergei. August 18, 2023. Who Was Alex Lowe? Retrieved on November 1, 2025 from https://endorfeen.com/alex_lowe/

[2] Woodward, Richard B. March 25, 2014. Nanny Strangest: On "Finding Vivian Maier". The Wall Street Journal. Retrieved on November 1, 2025 from https://www.wsj.com/articles/SB10001424052702303725404579461170488341910

[3] Asimov, Isaac. (1950) 2004. "Runaround." In I, Robot (The Isaac Asimov Collection ed.), 31–49. New York City: Doubleday.

[4] Sagan, Carl. 1980. *Cosmos*. New York, NY: Random House.

[5] Sagan, Carl. 1984. *Pale Blue Dot: A Vision of the Human Future in Space*. New York, NY: Random House.

# CHAPTER 14

# The Outer Pursuits – Connector, Culturist, Anthroguard, and Conservationist

THIS CHAPTER EXPLORES FOUR fundamental pursuits that define a meaningful life by looking outward, engaging with the world beyond the self. Here, purpose is not found in individual experience but in connection to others, culture, our species, and the natural world. They are the Connector, who values the richness of human interaction, forged bonds, and shared experiences, driven by an intrinsic need to build and nurture human connections; the Culturist, who acts as custodian of human heritage and is dedicated to safeguarding the rich tapestry of human culture; the Anthroguard, who is committed to ensuring the preservation and welfare of our species; and the Conservationist, who seeks to preserve the natural world, including all biological life. These are pursuits that find their meaning in an external source, ones that cannot be undertaken by an individual alone. These four types of pursuits are represented in one of the two arms of the Lucidus Pursuits (Figure 13.1), with the order roughly representing the scale of pursuit, from small (Connectors) to large (Conservationists). The structure of this chapter mirrors Chapter 13.

DOI: 10.1201/9781003711131-18

## CONNECTORS

### Building Bonds through Kindness

Fred Rogers (1928–2003), a soft-spoken television host from Pittsburgh, dedicated his life to nurturing human connections and fostering relationships through his show *Mister Rogers' Neighborhood* [1]. From 1968 to 2001, he welcomed children and adults into his gentle world, using simple puppets and heartfelt conversations to explore feelings from joy to fear. Each episode, he would slip on his cardigan, tie his sneakers, and speak directly to viewers, affirming their worth with unwavering sincerity. In a 1969 episode, amid racial tensions and segregated public pools, Fred invited François Clemmons, the African-American actor playing Officer Clemmons, to share a small wading pool on his show. This simple gesture defied the era's racial barriers, showing children and adults that kindness transcends color. Off-screen, Fred lived his message, writing personal letters to fans, comforting a grieving child at a hospital, or pausing to listen to strangers with full attention. His archive of over 900 episodes, filled with songs and stories, became a timeless gift, touching millions through reruns and tributes like the award-winning documentary *Won't You Be My Neighbor?* The Pittsburgh Children's Museum has a special section that recreates his show's set, where I used to take our kids to when they were young. His passion was connection itself, and each moment was a quiet celebration of shared humanity.

Fred Rogers was a vanguard Connector.

### Who Are the Connectors

Connectors are driven by an intrinsic need to build and nurture human relationships in an increasingly digital world. They are drawn to all aspects of connection, from family bonds and intimate friendships to communal ties, and they place a premium on values like fairness, trust, acceptance, and respect.

They view the universe as an intricate web of relationships, where every being is linked. Rather than seeing life as a stage for individual achievement, Connectors understand that their identity is co-created through interactions with others. For them, the fundamental questions of origin and purpose are answered not through individual introspection but through the shared experiences and emotional bonds that unite people.

Their ultimate goal is to foster and sustain a life rich in human connection. They aim to establish, nurture, and preserve bonds that enable close family, authentic friendships, and a strong sense of community.

Connectors prioritize goals that enhance collective well-being and culti-vate relationships where fairness, trust, and acceptance are the norm.

To achieve this, they embrace practices that promote active, positive engage-ment, while setting clear boundaries against behaviors that could erode trust. Rituals are particularly important, as they formalize and celebrate human connection, from seasonal festivals to the simple sharing of meals. Their decision-making is guided by empathy and mutual support, as they believe every interaction is an opportunity to build trust and strengthen belonging.

## CULTURIST

### Transformer of Korea's Culture

King Sejong the Great (1397–1450), a visionary Joseon ruler, devoted his life to enriching and preserving Korean culture and to nurturing his peo-ple's shared identity [2]. He created Hangul, a simple alphabet tailored to the Korean language to replace complex Chinese characters, so farmers, scholars, and children could read and write their own stories, ensuring that cultural wisdom could be passed down seamlessly through genera-tions. In doing so, Sejong not only preserved the essence of Korean culture but also encouraged its development. He worked closely with his people, sparking a cultural revival through music, literature, and science. He often walked among his subjects to hear their needs, determined to unite them through their heritage. His legacy, marked by the creation of Hangul and a steadfast commitment to Korean identity, lives on in Korea's language and pride, celebrated in museums and annual festivals.

Sejong was a vanguard Culturist.

### Who Are the Culturists

Culturists are dedicated to enriching and safeguarding the tapestry of human culture in an era increasingly dominated by DI. For them, the essence of being human is rooted in our cultural heritage, languages, tra-ditions, arts, and collective narratives. Their commitment is not just to preserve the past, but to nurture and develop it for future generations.

They believe human culture is the essence of who we are. For Culturists, the cosmos is an interconnected web of human stories and cultural lega-cies. Every myth, tradition, and work of art is a testament to what defines our species. They see cultural output, whether through music, literature, or rituals, as the unique fingerprint of human existence.

Their ultimate goal is the preservation and further development of human culture. This involves both maintaining the integrity of traditions and cultivating new expressions of cultural identity. Their lifelong goals revolve around fostering environments where traditions can flourish in the face of digital influence and ensuring that human culture remains the defining signature of our species.

To achieve this, they adopt practices that preserve the authenticity of cultural expression. They establish routines to educate younger generations and keep cultures alive, as well as rules to guard against cultural dilution. For Culturists, rituals are essential, serving to formalize and celebrate human connection, from seasonal festivals to traditional holidays. These practices not only honor the past but also create a sense of continuity and collective memory.

## ANTHROGUARD
### The Voice of Global Harmony

John Lennon (1940–1980) was a world-class artist and peace advocate who devoted his life to awakening and nurturing a global sense of understanding, unity, and peace. Through his music, words, and public life, he sought to dissolve the national and religious boundaries that divide us. With his iconic song *Imagine*, Lennon declared himself a dreamer of a harmonious world and invited everyone to join him so the shared dream could become reality. He walked with protestors, sang with the marginalized, and spoke out against injustice, as a fellow human yearning for harmony. In 1969, he and Yoko Ono staged the "Bed-Ins for Peace" in Amsterdam and Montreal during their honeymoon, knowing it would attract major global media coverage [3]. They sat in their hotel bed and invited the press to talk about peace, turning their honeymoon into a platform for anti-war activism and giving voice to a generation disillusioned by conflict. His legacy, marked by his unwavering commitment to peace and human dignity, lives on in voices that still sing *Imagine*, in murals and vigils across continents, and in movements that echo his call for a more loving and united world.

John Lennon was a vanguard Anthroguard.

### Who Are the Anthroguards

Anthroguards are committed to actively safeguarding and steering the ongoing evolution of humanity. They see themselves as the proactive custodians of our species' future. Their drive is rooted in a belief that our progress depends on our ability to preserve and advance our biological selves and everything associated with them.

They view the universe as more than just a collection of physical phenomena, they see it as intricately linked with the trajectory of human advancement. Their understanding of who they are is tied to humanity's unique position as the only known species with symbolic language, the species that created the powerful DI.

The ultimate objective for Anthroguards is the preservation and continuous advancement of our species. They set ambitious, forward-thinking goals to address existential challenges and opportunities for growth. Their minimum goal is to ensure humanity collectively maintains its biological identity as a species.

To achieve this, they use a combination of proactive initiatives and safeguards against forces that could derail progress. They promote active stewardship of human development through initiatives that enhance education, ethics, and critical thinking. They guard against divisive practices that could undermine social cohesion and actively monitor DI to ensure its advancement does not come at the cost of a diminished humanity. They seek experiences in policy forums and public advocacy to engage directly with the forces shaping the future.

## CONSERVATIONIST

### The Book That Gave Birth to Environmental Movement

Rachel Carson (1907–1964) devoted her life to awakening humanity's sense of kinship with the natural world and defending the delicate systems that sustain life on Earth. Through her work, she invited people to see nature as a living community to which we belong, worthy of wonder, respect, and protection. With her groundbreaking book *Silent Spring* [4], Carson exposed the hidden dangers of unchecked industrial growth such as pesticide use, revealing how chemicals like DDT were poisoning birds, fish, and entire ecosystems. She called for policy change and, more fundamentally, a new ethical paradigm that recognized the deep interdependence between humans and the environment. Carson faced intense opposition from powerful chemical companies, yet she stood firm and sparked a movement that led to the eventual ban of DDT in the United States and the birth of the modern environmental movement. Her legacy, marked by the protection of species and the awakening of environmental consciousness, lives on in national parks, clean air and water legislation, and the global rise of ecological stewardship. Her voice still echoes in every call to preserve what we cannot replace.

Carson was a vanguard Conservationist.

## Who Are the Conservationists

Conservationists are dedicated to preserving BI and the natural world, seeing themselves as custodians of the planet. They work to ensure all life is allowed to progress organically without damaging the delicate systems that sustain it.

They perceive the universe through the lens of intricate natural evolution. They believe that nature, over countless iterations, has honed the conditions for life to flourish on Earth. They see this as a miracle worthy of preservation and argue that radical human interference could disrupt this finely tuned equilibrium. To them, humanity does not have the right to change other BI and the natural world simply to serve its own purpose.

For Conservationists, the primary objective is to preserve the biological status quo and the natural environment, ensuring they remain largely unaltered. Their vision is not to halt progress but to ensure that advancement does not come at the cost of ill-conceived, disruptive change. They seek a state of equilibrium where human development is in harmony with natural evolution.

To achieve this, they advocate sustainable human development. They stand against behaviors that could disturb the natural order, such as radical genetic editing of BI. They maintain that interventions should be limited to those that are absolutely necessary, allowing nature to progress organically. They also seek experiences that create a deep connection with nature and other forms of life.

## THOUGHT EXPERIMENT: THE PURSUIT OF COLLECTIVE PURPOSE

Imagine you have the rare chance to sit with the four vanguards introduced in this chapter, the Connector, the Culturist, the Anthroguard, and the Conservationist. Each has dedicated their life to a cause larger than themselves: nurturing human bonds, safeguarding cultural heritage, protecting the human species, or defending the natural world. Yet you approach them not as a supporter, but as a skeptic armed with doubt. Your task is to question whether their chosen pursuit was truly meaningful. Could their energy have been better spent elsewhere?

This thought experiment has three parts for each vanguard:

The Challenge. Formulate a critique that strikes at the heart of their purpose. Raise sharp questions and highlight the limitations of their work. Why should we prize fragile human connections in a digital world? Is preserving culture not just clinging to the past? Why worry about humanity when it has survived and even prospered for millennia, enduring wave after wave of violence? Why sound the alarm over extinction when it has always been the rule rather than the exception, with countless species vanishing since life first appeared on Earth? In short, build the strongest case for why their pursuit was misguided, inconsequential, or obsolete.

The Rebuttal. Now give each vanguard the chance to answer in their own voice, drawing on their writings, actions, and legacy. How might Fred Rogers defend the value of kindness and connection, or Sejong the Great justify the creation of a shared language? How would John Lennon speak for the need to protect humanity from division, or Rachel Carson argue for the defense of ecosystems against unchecked human power? Let them push back, point by point, with the conviction and perspective that shaped their lives.

The Reflection. Finally, step back and reflect on what the exchange reveals. What do you learn by challenging these vanguards and then listening to their defense? How does this deepen your understanding of why people devote themselves to causes beyond the self, even when results seem uncertain or fragile? More importantly, how does it help you see why the pursuits of Connector, Culturist, Anthroguard, and Conservationist will remain essential pillars of meaning in Lucidus Society?

Through this exercise, you grapple with the question of collective purpose. By testing it with doubt, you discover what endures and perhaps what may guide your own path toward becoming a vanguard in service of something larger than yourself.

## REFERENCES

[1] Bianculli, David. (February 19, 2018). It's a beautiful 50th birthday for 'Mister Rogers' neighborhood. NPR. https://www.npr.org/2018/02/19/586180373/its-a-beautiful-50th-birthday-for-mister-rogers-neighborhood

[2] King Sejong the Great And The Golden Age of Korea. Retrieved on November 1, 2025 from https://asiasociety.org/education/king-sejong-great

[3] Enos, Elysha. April 21, 2019. 50th anniversary of John and Yoko's bed-in celebrated in Old Montreal. CBC News. Retrieved on November 1, 2025 from https://www.cbc.ca/news/canada/montreal/yoko-ono-exhibition-50-anniversary-bed-in-1.5105429

[4] Carson, Rachel. 1962. *Silent Spring*. Boston, MA: Houghton Mifflin Company.

# CHAPTER 15

# Envision and Enabling Your Personal Future – Becoming a Vanguard of *Homo lucidus*

## WISDOM FROM DESERT

Antoine de Saint-Exupéry, a French aviator and writer, wove his life's daring and introspection into timeless literary works. As a pioneering airmail pilot, he braved perilous routes across the Sahara and Andes, carrying mail across deserts, mountains, and oceans at a time when flight was still perilous, facing crashes and isolation that shaped his philosophy of resilience amid uncertainty. During World War II, serving in Free French reconnaissance missions until his mysterious disappearance in 1944, he channeled personal and global turmoil into *Citadelle* (published posthumously in 1948 as The *Wisdom of the Sands*). In Chapter LVI, his fictional desert chieftain declares, "As for the future, your task is not to predict it, but to enable it" [1]. Written amid war's chaos, this statement captures his conviction that the future is not predestined, but a construction project we take part in, stone by stone. He urges his readers not to wait passively for

DOI: 10.1201/9781003711131-19

tomorrow, but to shape it actively in the present, turning uncertainty into agency.

Your own personal future in Lucidus Society lies within your reach. In this final chapter, I offer suggestions on how you can envision the role you want to play in that society by learning from the vanguards of the eight Lucidus Pursuits. I also invite you to assess for yourself the societal and technological forces that will shape your path. Once you clarify both your vision and the road that could take you there, you can begin the journey of turning that vision into reality, step by step.

Finally, I challenge you to complete the last thought experiment, write a future history of yourself, as if you were already in 2045, looking back and recounting your personal biography from today to then.

## ENVISION WHO YOU WANT TO BECOME

If you already know with certainty who you want to become in 2045 and beyond, you can skip this section. For everyone else, one of the most effective ways to explore where your heart truly lies is through the vanguards of each pursuit type. Below are four steps to guide that process.

First is to seek. Begin by seeking out vanguards of any lucidus type that sparks even a faint interest in you. Chapters 13 and 14 described the defining traits of each pursuit and highlighted historical examples. I chose only vanguards who are no longer living so that the task of finding living, active vanguards falls to you. These contemporary figures are the ones whose pursuits you can observe and learn from directly.

Second is to study. Study these vanguards through secondary sources such as books. Books are long-form, immersive experiences, they force you to linger with an idea, a story, or a mind long enough for it to shift something within you. This might mean reading a vanguard's biography, their own writings, or a work that captures the philosophical or practical foundations of their pursuit. You should read what they did and why they did it, and let their logic and worldview challenge or inspire your own.

Third is to follow. Follow their actions if they are still active, through social media, public talks, interviews, or other accessible platforms. We live in an era where you can watch someone's journey unfold almost in real time. This is not voyeurism but an ongoing education in values and choices. The vanguards you follow need not be famous, but they should be authentic, with clear values, visible actions, and consistent presence. You should pay attention to what they say or do, how they navigate decisions, where they invest their energy, and what sacrifices they make. Long-term observation will reveal patterns and contexts that no book could convey.

Fourth is to participate. Try doing what the vanguards are doing. Even small, carefully chosen actions can often teach you more about yourself than any abstract reflection. The task does not need to be impressive, it only needs to demand effort, be tied to the real practices of the pursuit, and fall within your capability. If you feel alive when doing them, even while clumsy, uncertain, or exhausted, that is a sign of alignment. If you feel only emptiness or persistent resistance, that too is a sign.

You do not need to commit to a single pursuit. Most people will be drawn to several, some more strongly than others, and these inclinations may evolve over time. A dynamic, multifaceted pursuit profile is often desirable. What matters is resisting the urge to lock yourself prematurely into one identity. As Socrates urged, "Know thyself". Through seeking, studying, following, and participating, you will begin to uncover what makes you feel most alive, and from there, envision who you want to become in Lucidus Society beyond 2045.

## ASSESSING THE ROAD AHEAD

Knowing what you want to become sets the destination for your journey. The next step is to travel the road that will take you there. Unlike many other journeys, however, the road to 2045 is not straight. It will be marked by constant rerouting as major societal and technological disruptions unfold, reshaping how you can reach your destination. To enable your personal future, you must form your own assessments of these disruptions, when they might occur, how they might alter the path ahead, and plan your journey accordingly.

These assessments should be specific and based on your personal judgment. For example, ask yourself when it might become possible for a human to be developed in an artificial womb and brought to birth, and how this will affect social structure. General speculation is not enough. What matters is your own best estimation, anchored in your understanding and reasoning, and it is much more likely you will act on such forecasts if these forecasts are made by you. Specific, personal forecasts make this assessment relevant and actionable as you chart your path forward.

In a 1964 BBC Horizon interview, science fiction author and futurist Arthur C. Clarke issued a warning that still resonates:

If what I say seems to you completely reasonable, then I will have failed completely. Only if what I am about to tell you appears absolutely unbelievable, have we any chance of visualizing the future as it really will happen.

[2]

Clarke captured a persistent human flaw in forecasting: our tendency to play it safe, imagining futures that look much like the present, only slightly improved. Such reasonable visions are often the least likely to come true because they are constrained by assumptions based on today's world.

The disruptions that truly reshape our world usually begin as ideas that seem absurd. This does not mean indulging in fantasy. Your assessment must remain anchored in plausible evolutions of society and technology, based on the trajectories already visible today. But it does require stretching beyond the obvious. To prepare for the road ahead, you must step past what feels reasonable and dare to envision futures that, though daring or even unbelievable now, may be the very ones that materialize.

In 2024, I shared Clarke's insights with several groups of senior executives from diverse industries, including many C-level leaders. I asked them to identify major societal and technological disruptions that mattered to them personally or professionally, and to forecast the probability of each disruption occurring by 2035. Table 15.1 presents a selection of their forecasts as an illustration of the road assessment task you need to undertake. Each forecast shown in the table was generated by one executive group, with each group consisting of roughly 60–80 participants. For every disruption, the table reports both the average probability assigned by all executives in that group and the distribution of forecasts across five probability ranges: 0%–20%, 21%–40%, 41%–60%, 61%–80%, and 81%–100% from that group.

We can draw several noteworthy observations even from this small set of forecasts. First, the disruptions identified are sweeping in scope, touching nearly every dimension of society and technology. Second, the average probabilities assigned to these drastic disruptions are high enough to merit serious attention and action. Third, the variation across executives is huge: some view a disruption as almost certain, while others see it as highly unlikely. The difference in opinions is expected, as Clarke's rule reminds us that correct predictions often appear unreasonable at first. A forecast that everybody can agree on will most likely be too conservative. These observations reveal that informed leaders already acknowledge

TABLE 15.1    Examples of Forecasting Probabilities of Major Societal and Technological Disruptions Happening by 2035

| Major Disruptions Happening by 2035 | Average Forecasted Probability | Distribution of Forecasts across Five Probability Ranges | | | | |
|---|---|---|---|---|---|---|
| | | 0%–20% | 21%–40% | 41%–60% | 61%–80% | 81%–100% |
| Flying cars widely used | 46% | 35% | 16% | 12% | 21% | 16% |
| Malignant tumors largely curable | 70% | 5% | 9% | 21% | 33% | 32% |
| 30% of people choosing robots as life partners | 39% | 49% | 9% | 18% | 11% | 14% |
| Artificial womb babies a reality | 49% | 26% | 18% | 25% | 12% | 19% |
| Disappearance of schools | 24% | 56% | 19% | 15% | 10% | 0% |
| One-third of urban youth mainly in the metaverse | 39% | 41% | 15% | 21% | 16% | 7% |
| Mars migrants surpassing 5,000 | 36% | 47% | 12% | 21% | 7% | 12% |

dramatic changes ahead, and they assign nontrivial probabilities to them, even if their individual views diverge widely.

More importantly, to the extent feasible, you should act on what you believe. After my discussions with these executives, I found that only a few had made any strategic adjustments, in their personal lives, professional development, or their firms, to prepare for or capitalize on the disruptions they themselves considered highly probable by 2035 (with forecasted probability above 80%). There is little value in assessing the road ahead if you continue to follow your existing routines regardless of how dramatically the world is expected to change.

## VISION WITH ACTION

There is a famous Japanese proverb: "Vision without action is a daydream, and action without vision is a nightmare". Both extremes are dangerous.

To dream of a future without grounding it in concrete steps is to live in illusion, while acting without a clear vision risks being swept along by noise, urgency, or the agendas of others.

Your task, therefore, is to hold both vision and action together. The vision sets your destination, clarifying what kind of person you want to become and what role you wish to play in Lucidus Society. The action is not just about moving forward, it must be shaped by your best assessment of the major societal and technological disruptions that lie ahead. If you foresee disruptions in health, education, work, relationships, or even how humans come into the world, then your plans must adapt accordingly. Otherwise, you risk preparing for a road that will no longer exist soon.

Clarity of vision keeps you from drifting aimlessly, while action informed by disruption-awareness ensures your steps are relevant and future-proof. When you unite the two, you create a genuine opportunity to enable the future you have envisioned.

## THOUGHT EXPERIMENT: A BIOGRAPHY FROM 2045

Future histories are imaginative narratives that describe tomorrow as though it had already happened. They are not forecasts, but creative exercises that help us think more clearly about where we are headed and what choices might shape the path. Writers like H.G. Wells and Isaac Asimov used this method to envision technologies, societies, and ways of living long before they became real.

Now it is your turn to apply this method, not to the world at large, but to yourself.

### Your Assignment

Write a personal future history, a biography composed in the year 2045, looking back on your life between now and then. You should tell the story as if you were narrating your own journey, reflecting on the choices, challenges, and milestones that brought you here.

The point is not to predict exactly what will happen. It is to enable the future you want by shaping it in words so you can begin laying its foundation today. Your life may not unfold exactly as you write it, but by giving it form now, you give yourself both direction and agency.

### Writing Suggestions

Tell It as a Story. Bring your imagined life to the page with vivid detail, mixing the ordinary with the extraordinary. For example:

- Career & Learning: How did you adapt to shifts in work, society, or technology? What new skills did you master?

- Family & Relationships: How did you nurture love, friendships, and human connection as the decades passed?

- Experiences & Adventures: What travels, collaborations, creative projects, or acts of service gave your life meaning?

- Challenges & Resilience: What obstacles did you face, and how did you grow stronger by overcoming them?

Write as if it Already Happened. Step into 2045 and use the past tense, as though you are reflecting from that vantage point. This shift in perspective helps you embody the mindset of someone who has already lived the life you want to create. For example:

- "In 2030, I decided to leave my comfort zone and…"

- "By 2034, I had finally reached a balance between…"

- "Looking back, I realize the turning point was when…"

Keep it Aspirational, not Fantastical. This is not a checklist or a resume, it is the story of a life worth striving toward. Be bold and honest about what matters most to you. At the same time, ground your future biography in plausible trajectories of social and technological change, just as you have assessed earlier in this chapter.

## REFERENCES

[1] Antoine de Saint-Exupéry. 1948. *The Wisdom of the Sands*, trans. Stuart Gilbert. New York: Harcourt Brace and Co., p. 50.
[2] BBC Archive. 1964. https://www.youtube.com/watch?v=YwELr8ir9qM

# Epilogue

## *To Prepare for the Future, Understand the Past*

A T THIS JUNCTURE IN human history, a deliberate return to the past can help you prepare for the future. I invite you to select a civilization that no longer exists as a political entity, preferably one dating back at least a millennium, and study its trajectory in depth. Examine its rise, its era of growth and stability, and finally its decline and demise, with special attention to how its intellectual and cultural legacies were preserved, diffused, or even expanded after its demise. The Roman Empire and the Han Dynasty, for example, could serve as such instructive cases, both contemporaneous at their zenith, with one dominating the Mediterranean and Western Europe, and the other dominating East Asia. You can draw upon historical records, archaeological findings, and scholarly analyses, and, when possible, retrace the events in the very places where they unfolded, to reconstruct this arc as comprehensively as possible. Immersing yourself in the legacies of past civilizations gives perspective when the world around you accelerates and resilience when institutions falter. It also sharpens your judgment of what is timeless versus what is transient, helping you focus on and pursue things that will endure in Lucidus Society.

Bon voyage! The journey ahead will be turbulent yet exhilarating. By making it to the end of this book, you have shown curiosity, initiative, critical thinking, and a commitment to learning and adaptation, qualities that will help you navigate the road ahead.

I look forward to seeing you at the grand celebration in 2045.

DOI: 10.1201/9781003711131-20

# Index

For Product Safety Concerns and Information please contact our EU
representative GPSR@taylorandfrancis.com
Taylor & Francis Verlag GmbH, Kaufingerstraße 24, 80331 München, Germany

www.ingramcontent.com/pod-product-compliance
Lightning Source LLC
Chambersburg PA
CBHW070716220326
41598CB00024BA/3190

9 781041 192411